Murder Most Vile
Volume Fifteen
18 Truly Shocking
Murder Cases

Robert Keller

Please Leave Your Review of This Book At
http://bit.ly/kellerbooks

ISBN-13: 978-1545264348
ISBN-10: 1545264341

© 2017 by Robert Keller

robertkellerauthor.com

Table of Contents

Scream

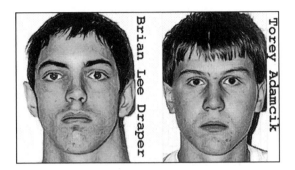

When legendary horror director Wes Craven released the teen slasher movie Scream in 1996, he probably had no idea how successful it was going to become, spawning a franchise that has grossed over $600 million in revenue. The plot after all, is hardly original. A group of high school students is terrorized by a masked killer who stalks and kills them one by one. When the murderer's identity is eventually revealed, he turns out to be not one, but two of their classmates, working together. Director Craven has admitted that the story was inspired by the real crimes of notorious serial killer Danny Rolling, alias The Gainesville Ripper. What is less well-known is that the movie itself inspired a particularly bloody murder.

Brian Draper and Torey Adamcik were a couple of apparently normal 16-year-olds, attending Pocatello High School in the city of Pocatello, Idaho. Torey had grown up in the area, while Brian had moved there recently from Utah with his family. The two were soon firm friends, drawn together by their mutual love of films, particularly horror movies. Torey in fact had ambitions of attending film school after graduation and had dreams of becoming a movie director. He was seldom, if ever seen without his video camera, shooting random footage and sometimes conducting impromptu interviews with his fellow students.

Of the two Torey was the more popular among his peers, Brian the more introverted. But they did have a few mutual acquaintances, notably Cassie Jo Stoddart and her boyfriend Matt Beckham. Like Brian and Torey, Cassie was in her junior year at Pocatello High and she and Matt were on friendly terms with the boys. What Cassie could not have imagined was that Brian and Torey were planning a massacre, with her the intended victim.

Where exactly this diabolical scheme had its genesis is difficult to fathom. After the event, Brian and Torey would both play the innocent and try to shift the blame to the other. But there is a substantial body of evidence to suggest that they were equally culpable. They certainly brought out the worst in one another, Torey with his slasher movie obsession and Brian with his admiration of Eric Harris and Dylan Klebold, the Columbine High School shooters. What we know is that in the months leading up to the massacre, they began shooting video footage in which they candidly discussed their worldview and their ambitions to become serial killers.

The video makes for disturbing viewing. In it, one or the other plays the role of interviewer while the other answers questions. Giggly and jovial, they share with the camera their Nietzsche-inspired views - that good and evil do not exist; that murder is only wrong because the law says so and that they, as superior human beings should be entitled to kill lesser individuals. They discuss the killers who they admire, dismissing Ted Bundy and the Hillside Stranglers as "amateurs" and honing in on Ed Gein as the ideal (even if they incorrectly attribute the crimes of Ed Kemper to Gein). And perhaps most chillingly, they describe the killing spree that they are going to carry out, talking about the time they've spent staking out potential victims and honing in eventually on Cassie Jo Stoddart and Matt Beckham. "They're our friends but we have to make sacrifices," Draper says into the camera. "So, um, I feel tonight is the night and I feel really weird and stuff. I feel like I want to kill somebody. Uh, I know that's not normal but what the hell."

That particular clip was recorded on September 21, 2006. By then, Draper and Adamcik's plans for mass slaughter were already well evolved. Three weeks earlier, Adamcik had called an 18-year-old friend named Joe Lucero and asked if he would buy some knives for him. Lucero had agreed and the two of them, together with Draper had gone to a local pawn shop and purchased four hunting knives for $45.

But the murder would not take place on September 21, probably because Cassie Jo Stoddart's parents were at home. The would-be killers then staked out the house of another potential victim before deciding that there was too much risk involved. They then called it a night. Their tilt at infamy would have to wait.

The following day, September 22, 2006, Cassie Jo Stoddart was due to housesit at her uncle's residence on Whispering Cliffs Drive. Adamcik and Draper got to hear of these plans at school when Cassie invited them to hang out with her and Matt that evening. Adamcik's video diary for that day contains one innocent and yet, in retrospect, chilling clip. It shows Cassie standing at her locker in the school hallway. Draper is filming and picks her up on camera. "Hey look, it's Cassie," he says, "Hello Cassie."

"Hello," Cassie replies smiling and waving at the camera.

"I'm getting you on tape," Draper giggles. "Say hi please."

"Hi," Cassie says smiling.

Within twelve hours of that segment being filmed, Cassie Jo Stoddart would be brutally slain by the youth behind the camera and his warped cohort.

Adamcik and Draper arrived at the Whispering Cliffs residence at around 7 p.m. on the evening of Friday, September 22. They spent around two hours chatting and joking with the two young people they intended killing. Then at around nine, Adamcik abruptly announced that they had to leave. Some fifteen minutes later the power at the home went out. That frightened Cassie and so she asked Matt if he could stay the night. Matt then phoned his parents and asked for permission to sleep over. His mom however said no and confirmed her prior arrangement to pick him up at 10:30. By the time she did so, the electricity had been restored and Cassie was feeling slightly less anxious. Little did she know that it had been Adamcik and Draper who had tampered with the power supply and that they were at that very moment hiding in the dark and watching the house. About half an hour after Matt Beckham departed, the lights went out again and this time the killers crept forward, gripping their recently acquired blades.

Cassie Jo Stoddart's body was not discovered until her uncle and his family returned home on Sunday evening and walked in on a bloodbath. The subsequent autopsy would reveal the true horrific extent of the murder. Cassie had been stabbed thirty times, with twelve of the wounds considered "potentially fatal." The pathologist also determined that two weapons had been used in the attack, one with a serrated edge, the other non-serrated. In view of the defense both killers would soon raise, this was a vital piece of evidence.

And tracking down those killers would be a relatively straightforward task. After Matt Beckham revealed that Draper and Adamcik had been at the house on the night of the murder they were questioned as potential witnesses. However, their answers to questions asked by investigators soon roused suspicion and before long they were elevated to the head of the suspect list.

Both however insisted that they knew nothing about the murder. According to them, they'd gone to a local movie theater to watch a film called Pulse. They were even able to provide ticket stubs, although neither seemed to have the slightest idea what the movie was actually about. Caught out in that lie, Draper changed his story. He now said that he and Adamcik had agreed to use the movie as an alibi. They had actually been out breaking into cars.

This admission was an immediate red flag to investigators. Experience told them that criminals hardly ever admit to a crime unless it is to cover up a more serious offense. Moreover, there had been no reports of burglarized vehicles in the area in which Draper claimed to have been operating. Convinced more than ever that Draper and Adamcik were lying, the investigators increased the pressure.

It was Draper who cracked first. During the course of his third interview on Wednesday, September 27, 2006, he admitted that he and Adamcik had gone back to the house after Beckham had left. They'd entered, he said, through a door which they'd deliberately unlocked earlier in the evening. According to Draper their intention had been to give Cassie a scare. But then Adamcik had drawn a knife and started stabbing Cassie. Draper initially denied hurting Cassie but he later admitted to stabbing her in the leg and chest. He'd only done so, he said, because Adamcik had threatened to kill him if he refused.

Draper also agreed to show police where he and Adamcik had disposed of the murder weapons and later that afternoon led a contingent of detectives and crime scene investigators to a location at Black Rock Canyon. Here several items were recovered, including bloodstained clothing, latex gloves, three daggers and a

Sony videotape. An attempt had been made to damage the tape but a police expert was able to recover the recording, which included some of the material mentioned earlier in this article. Particularly telling however, was a segment apparently filmed directly after the murder.

Draper and Adamcik are in a car driving, with Adamcik at the wheel and Draper holding the video camera.

Draper: "We just killed Cassie! We just left her house. This is not a fucking joke."

Adamcik: "I'm shaking."

Draper: "I stabbed her in the throat and I saw her lifeless body. It just disappeared. Dude, I just killed Cassie!"

Adamcik: "Oh my God!"

Draper: "Oh, oh fuck. That felt like it wasn't even real. I mean it went by so fast."

Adamcik: "Shut the fuck up. We gotta get our act straight."

Draper: "It's okay. We'll just buy movie tickets now."

Adamcik: "Okay."

Brian Draper and Torey Adamcik were tried separately for the murder of Cassie Jo Stoddart. At trial, each of them attempted to shift the blame to the other and to portray himself as having been coerced to participate in the murder. The videos, so meticulously compiled by these wannabe filmmakers told a different story, proving that each was equally liable. The juvenile killers were both found guilty and received identical sentences, life in prison without the possibility of parole. They are currently incarcerated at the Idaho State Correctional Institution near Kuna, Idaho. Appeals to the US Supreme court by both killers have been denied.

Moon Madness

Peter Griffiths

It was 1 a.m. on the morning of Saturday, May 15, 1948, and Nurse
Gwen Humphreys was doing her rounds at the Queen's Park
Hospital in Blackburn, Lancashire. The young nurse had been
working the graveyard shift for a number of months now but she
really didn't mind, particularly on a night like this with a full moon
spilling in feathered light through the porch doors. To Gwen, it
transformed the drab surroundings into some magical kingdom
and that was particularly true of Ward CH3, the children's ward,
her favorite. She found it hard to suppress a smile as she walked
the aisle between the beds and surveyed their cherub-like faces.
Sleep and moonlight she decided, had the power to turn even the
most mischievous of little monsters into an angel.

Nurse Humphreys was not immediately alarmed when she noticed
that the door leading out onto the porch stood ajar. Many of these
doors had faulty latches and some were known to be dislodged by
the slightest of breezes. She walked silently to the end of the room
and shut it, re-engaging the catch. It was then that she noticed the
muddy footprints on the floor and her breath caught in her throat.
The trail of mud led across the highly-polished floor and
terminated at a particular cot further back in the room. Her alarm
growing, the nurse walked quickly towards the cot and found that
it was empty, although still warm to the touch. Had its occupant,

four-year-old June Devaney got up to use the bathroom? Nurse Humphreys knew immediately that that was not the case. The cot's side rail was still up and there was no way the little girl could have climbed over that. No, someone had lifted her out of the bed, the same someone who had left muddy footprints leading into and out of the ward. Humphreys ran immediately to alert the ward sister. When a search by hospital staff failed to turn up any sign of the missing child, the sister called the police.

Before long, the hospital grounds were swarming with uniformed officers beating the bushes and calling out to June. Some carried flashlights but for the most part those instruments were superfluous. The moon was so bright on that cloudless morn that it easily lit their path. And that path was to lead to a tragic discovery two hours later. June Devaney's broken body was found in the shadows of a boundary wall. Her nightgown was stained with blood and it was evident that she had sustained horrendous head injuries. A smear of red on the wall suggested how those injuries might have occurred and the medical examiner would later confirm that theory. June's killer had held her by the feet and smashed her head against the brickwork. Before he'd carried out that bestial act, he'd committed another. The little girl had been raped.

As word of the horrific murder began seeping out to the community, a sense of outrage, shock and disbelief descended on the town. Chief Constable Looms of the Blackburn Police was left with a difficult decision to make. Should he allow his own detectives to carry out the investigation or should he call in Scotland Yard? The latter course was likely to be unpopular with his men, who like most regional police forces resented interference from London. On the other hand, people were extremely angry and were demanding swift justice. Failure to deliver that justice was likely to have dire consequences. It might even lead to public unrest. Correctly judging the mood of the community, Looms decided to call on the Metropolitan Police for help. The officer who was dispatched was the legendary Detective Chief Inspector Jack Capstick.

Capstick was an anomaly during that era, a senior police officer who had not had the benefit of a public school education and had risen through the ranks. Yet he was esteemed on both sides of the legal divide. Criminals respected him as hard but fair, while his subordinates adored him. Those in the upper echelons might not have been that keen on the unconventional detective but those objections were mainly political in nature. Capstick was no respecter of rank. He was however an exceptionally intuitive detective with a phenomenal arrest rate. Now his job was to bring a uniquely depraved killer to book and he dared not fail.

Arriving in Blackburn with his trusted lieutenant Detective Inspector Wilf 'Flapper' Daws, Capstick got immediately to work. First he viewed the body, an experience that apparently brought the hard-as-nails detective to tears. Then he reviewed what little evidence there was. The killer had apparently gained access to the ward by pushing up against the faulty door. He'd entered on stockinged feet leaving the unique trail of muddy footprints. No one knew why he'd passed by other children and abducted June Devaney, but it was evident that he'd lifted the child from her bed and carried her from the ward into the hospital grounds. There, he'd raped and then killed her.

There was one other clue and it was a vital one. A large medicine bottle had been left under June's bed, apparently placed there by the killer. Several fingerprints had been lifted from the bottle and all but one had been matched to hospital staff. Capstick was convinced that this print belonged to the murderer. However, a search of police records returned no match. Whoever had killed June Devaney had never been arrested before. Capstick however was convinced that he would kill again unless he was caught soon. He therefore decided to take a calculated risk, one that might cost him his career if it didn't pay off.

Capstick's idea was to fingerprint every man over the age of sixteen who had been in Blackburn on the night of the murder. When the plan was first touted it was met with a barrage of resistance, first from Capstick's superiors in London and then from officials and community leaders in Blackburn. Common citizens too, were angered by the implication that they might be considered suspects in this brutal crime. Capstick though was unmoved by the opposition and announced his intention to press ahead. The locals were placated by an assurance that all of the prints would be destroyed once the process was completed. From colleagues at The Yard though, Capstick heard whisperings that he was done if his gamble failed to deliver dividends.

And so the process of fingerprinting every adult male resident of the Lancashire town began. It was a mammoth undertaking, one that required the full-time attention of twenty officers over a period of two months. Using the electoral register, the officers eventually compiled a database of 46,000 sets of fingerprints.

Not one of those matched the prints found on the medicine bottle.

Capstick was perplexed. He'd been certain that the killer was someone with local knowledge, someone who'd known how to get into the hospital grounds and make his way to the wards. He slept hardly a wink that night, revisiting his logic again and again. Had he been wrong? Was the killer some transient who had committed the atrocity and then moved on? The more he thought about it, the more he became convinced that that wasn't the case. What had he missed then?

Eventually, in the early morning, hours it came to him. His officers had used the electoral register to determine who should be fingerprinted. What if the killer he was hunting wasn't on the roll? That got him thinking about who might not be included and led him to his eureka moment. Military serviceman who had been discharged since the last update - they wouldn't be included. Hauling himself out of bed at four in the morning, Capstick made a call to Scotland Yard. By noon that day he had a new much shorter list. By evening he had his match. The print belonged to 22-year-old Peter Griffiths, a young serviceman who'd been discharged from the Welsh Guards just months before.

Griffiths was immediately arrested and brought in for questioning. He initially denied any involvement in the murder and expressed outrage that he was accused of sexual violence against a child. But he could provide no explanation for how his fingerprints had ended up on the medicine bottle and he was unable to provide an alibi, saying that he could not remember what he'd been doing on the night in question.

Capstick however was a skilled interrogator. To him, the young man's body language told a different story. The way he refused to make eye contact, the way he kept clenching and unclenching his fists, the quiver in his voice as he made his replies, all of these were clear signs of inner turmoil. Capstick started playing on Griffiths need to unburden himself, assuring him that he'd feel better once he got it off his chest. Eventually it worked. Griffiths dropped his chin to his chest and said in a barely audible voice. "You're right. I killed her."

Over the hours that followed, Griffiths retold the events of that dreadful night. He said that he'd been out drinking and had visited several pubs, consuming a considerable amount of beer and rum. After closing time, he'd gone for a walk to clear his head and had ended up outside the hospital grounds. He did not remember scaling the fence but he did remember standing outside the children's ward, taking off his boots and then entering. Over the next few minutes he'd walked through the wards and several smaller rooms, on one occasion hiding in the shadows to avoid being discovered by a passing nurse. He'd then decided to leave but as he was walking back through the children's ward, he accidently bumped up against a bed and its occupant started crying.

Griffiths said that he initially went to comfort the child but then for some reason decided to pick her up and carry her outside. There he laid her down on the ground but when she started whimpering again he lost his temper and banged her head against the wall. He then left her there and went to retrieve his shoes which were still outside the ward. When he returned he noticed that the child wasn't moving and realized she must be dead. He then scaled the fence again and walked home. The child's death had plagued him ever since. "I hope I get what I deserve," he added tearfully.

The confession had made no mention of the rape and had played down the monstrous way in which little June Devaney's life had been ended. But Capstick didn't need Griffiths to elaborate on that. The medical examiner's testimony would leave the jury in no doubt as to the truly horrific nature of this crime.

The trial of Peter Griffiths began at Lancaster Assizes on October 15, before Mr. Justice Oliver. Griffiths entered a not guilty plea, with his defense attorney citing his low intelligence and producing an expert to testify that Griffiths was suffering from schizophrenia. That perhaps was the only strategy available to the child murderer but it was never one that was likely to succeed. Not when an entire community was baying for justice.

In the end, it took the jury just 23 minutes to return a verdict of guilty. Judge Oliver then donned the black cap and delivered a sentence of death by hanging. Peter Griffiths was executed on the gallows at Walton Prison on November 19, 1948. His executioner Albert Pierrepoint later recorded that he "died like a soldier."

Guilty as Sin

Growing up as a pastor's daughter can be tough on a girl, especially a pretty 18-year-old like Wanda Dworecki. Raised in Camden, New Jersey in the late 1930's, the petite redhead lived a somewhat insular lifestyle. Her father, the Reverend Walter Dworecki was a strict disciplinarian who treated his daughter like an indentured servant. Ever since her mother had died a year earlier, Wanda had been required to keep house, tend to her two younger siblings and obey her father in all things. Naturally compliant, she seldom complained.

But what the Reverend Dworecki did not know about his daughter was that she was a passionate young woman. In the parlance of the day, Wanda was "boy crazy" and likely to go off with any young man who gave her the eye. Opportunities for such liaisons were of course extremely limited, since her father kept her continuously under his watchful gaze. But Wanda found a way, whether it was a snuggle in the back of a movie theater during a matinee or a kiss in the church parking lot while her father was at the pulpit, she found a way. On two terrifying occasions, these stolen moments almost got her killed.

The first of those incidents happened on February 14, 1939. Wanda had been given permission to escort a neighbor's 11-year-old daughter Helen to the local cinema. As they approached their destination, a young man stopped beside them in a green coupe. He rolled down his window and gave Wanda a dazzling smile. "You girls need a ride?" he said.

"Maybe," Wanda replied, returning his grin with interest.

"Hop in then," the man said, stretching behind him to pop the rear door. Wanda looked uncertainly at Helen but the child was already scrambling into the back seat. Wanda then slid in beside the driver and he pulled away from the curb and edged the vehicle into traffic. About ten minutes later the driver pulled the car to a stop on a quiet stretch of road outside the city limits. Taking this to mean that he wanted to start necking, Wanda was about to inform him that she wasn't about to get into that with a child in the car when he suddenly shot out a hand and grabbed her by the throat. Panic-stricken, Wanda lashed out with her nails, raking his face. But the man kept squeezing, increasing the pressure. Had Helen not started screaming at that moment, Wanda might well have been killed. She and Helen were later picked up walking along the road by a Sherriff's deputy who drove her to the hospital and then called her father.

Wanda's injuries were fortunately not serious. But the whole episode earned her a tongue lashing from her father who admonished her for accepting a ride from a stranger. Wanda promised that she'd never do it again. Within months she'd broken that promise, with even more dire consequences.

Peter Schewchuck was a troubled young man who had been in and out of various juvenile facilities and had recently been arrested for car theft. The Reverend Dworecki however saw something in the 20-year-old and decided to give him a home and a second chance in life. Someone else also saw something in Peter. He was a handsome young man, tall and sandy-haired and Wanda was instantly attracted. It wasn't long before they were sleeping together. When the reverend found out, he ejected Schewchuck from his house.

But Wanda and Peter continued to see one another, usually when Rev. Dworecki made one of his frequent visits to Philadelphia. It was on the eve of one of those visits that she got a call from Peter asking her to meet him.

Wanda was beside herself with excitement. As soon as her father drove away she rushed upstairs, slipped into her best dress and hastily applied her makeup. Then she left the house and hurried to the corner of Broadway where Peter had arranged to meet her. Except Peter wasn't there. Instead, she found three young men sitting in a parked car.

"You the preacher's daughter?" one of them asked. Wanda nodded nervously and peered into the vehicle.

"I was supposed to meet my friend here," she said. "We're going to a party."

"Yeah, ol' Pete sent us to get you," the driver said, flipping open the door. "Get on board."

"Gee, I don't know..." Wanda said, her previous experience still fresh in her mind. "Maybe, I..."

"You want to go to this party or what?" the driver snapped.

"I... I... guess so," Wanda said hesitantly.

"Then get in. Time's a-wasting."

And so Wanda got into the vehicle and it was the worst decision she'd made in her short life. She was driven to a field near Swedesboro, dragged from the car and then brutally beaten and gang raped. Then her attackers left her lying in the dirt while they drove off laughing.

At around 11 o'clock that night, a farmer in Auburn woke to the sound of someone groaning in pain outside his front door. He went to investigate and found Wanda Dworecki lying on his porch naked, her face so severely beaten that she could barely see out of her eyes. The man immediately called an ambulance and Wanda was rushed to hospital, where doctors assessed the extent of her injuries and called the police. They in turn called Rev. Dworecki and told him that his daughter had been savagely attacked. The reverend was at first incredulous, saying that his daughter was asleep upstairs. But after checking her bed and finding it empty, he rushed to the hospital to be by Wanda's side.

Wanda would remain hospitalized for over a month, during which the police carried out an extensive search for the rapists. They tried also to find Peter Schewchuck, even though Wanda insisted that he'd had nothing to do with the attack and Rev. Dworecki also vouched for his good name. In the end both searches, the search for the rapists and the search for Schewchuck came up empty.

Eventually Wanda was discharged and allowed to come home. But while some of her physical injuries may have healed, the mental ones had left her a shadow of her former self. The once vivacious young woman now shuffled around the house like an old maid and jumped at every sound. She seldom spoke, seldom smiled and had to be forced to eat by her father. The savage attack had taken a toll on the reverend too. He seemed wan and pale and often lost in thought.

But at least he was going easier on his daughter. In early June he returned from one of his Philadelphia visits and excitedly announced to Wanda that he had bumped into Peter Schewchuck and had invited him to visit her at the rectory. Wanda was excited by this news too. For the first time in months her father saw a spark in her eye.

And so Wanda's romance with Peter was rekindled, this time with her father's blessing. Over the next month he visited regularly, sometimes several times a week. And if Rev. Dworecki knew that he and Wanda were intimate during this time, he made no complaint. All he wanted it seemed was his daughter's happiness.

On August 7, 1939, Rev. Dworecki had another surprise for his daughter. "I saw Peter in town today," he told her. "And I gave him permission to take you to the movies tonight."

Wanda was at first uncertain about the idea. She wanted to be with Peter of course, but her ordeal was still fresh in her mind and the idea of being outdoors at night terrified her. Her father however was adamant. She needed to start getting her life together, he said, and there was no time like the present. Besides, it was only a short walk to the corner of Haddon Street where Peter would meet her at 8 p.m. Wanda eventually agreed and left the house at around 7:45. A short time after she departed, Rev. Dworecki announced to his other children that he was heading to Philadelphia to visit a parishioner.

It rained heavily that night, the downpour lasting until after midnight when Rev. Dworecki got home. Then a check of the bedrooms told him that Wanda had not returned from her date with Peter. A short while later, he woke his children in a state of obvious distress and told them that he was going out to search for their sister. That search would continue through the night without any success. Eventually at around 8 o'clock, a mentally and physically exhausted Rev. Dworecki walked into a Camden police station and reported Wanda missing.

But by then Wanda had already been found and the news was not good. Earlier that morning, a farmer had gone to investigate a blockage in a drainage ditch and had been shocked to find the corpse of a young woman lying in the weeds. The man had run to the road and flagged down a motorist who had then alerted the police. One of the first officers at the scene had recognized the victim. He knew her from the gang rape case a few months earlier.

The police once again had dreadful, tragic news to deliver to Rev. Dworecki about his daughter. Wanda had been strangled and then bludgeoned to death with a rock, the heavy blows shattering her skull. There was evidence too that she had been sexually assaulted.

But at least this time the police had a suspect. While questioning an inconsolable Rev. Dworecki, they learned that Wanda had gone that night to the movies with her friend Peter Schewchuck. Dworecki was asked to give a description of the suspect and said that Schewchuck was short, strongly-built and dark-haired. While an APB was distributed for a man matching that description the case was assigned to one of New Jersey's top investigators, Lieutenant W.L. Dube of the State Police.

Lieutenant Dube had never been one to prejudge a case. Peter Schewchuck was undoubtedly the main suspect but that did not mean that Dube was going to disregard other avenues of investigation. He began looking into the backgrounds of the other players and was astonished at what he found on Rev. Dworecki.

The pastor was a long way short of the paragon of virtue he pretended to be. In fact, he was a suspect in a number of arson-for-profit cases and there were also questions regarding the sudden death of his wife, on whom Dworecki had taken out a $2,500 policy. The reverend incidentally, had also insured Wanda to the tune of $2,695. That policy included a double indemnity clause meaning that the payout was doubled if Wanda died as the result of an accident or homicide. Quite aside from this, it appeared that Dworecki was a well-known face in Philadelphia's red-light district. And he wasn't there to preach to the girls.

None of this of course meant that Dworecki was in any way involved in his daughter's murder. However when Dube questioned the other Dworecki children, another anomaly emerged. The reverend had described Peter Schewchuck to police as short, well-built and dark-haired, the description that the children gave was the polar opposite – tall, slim and with sandy hair. Why would Dworecki have given a description that was so far off the mark, Dube wondered? The answer was simple. He didn't want Schewchuck to be found.

With that motive established, Dube redoubled his efforts to find the elusive Peter. He even roped in the help of Schewchuck's father, informing him that the longer his son stayed on the lam the worse it would be for him. Three weeks later Schewchuck Sr. phoned the police and Peter was arrested.

Initially, Peter denied any involvement in Wanda's death. He admitted meeting her that night but said that while they were on their way to the movie, Wanda had dumped him and gone off with two men in a car. That story was quite obviously a lie. Given Wanda's recent trauma, it was highly unlikely that she'd get into a vehicle with two strangers. Dube said as much to Schewchuck and then continued pressing until the young man finally cracked.

"Okay, okay, I killed her, but he made me do it."

"He? Who is he?" Dube asked, already knowing the answer.

"Reverend Dworecki," Schewchuck said. "He told me that he'd have me arrested for statutory rape if I didn't do it."

Schewchuck then went on to describe how Dworecki had pestered and cajoled him for months to kill Wanda. He'd told Peter that Wanda was pregnant with his child. If it were made public they would both be ruined. Dworecki would lose his congregation and Schewchuck would go to prison for having sex with a minor. Eventually Schewchuck agreed to do it. On the night of the murder, he and Wanda had not gone to the movies but to the Camden High School athletic fields where they planned to make love. While Wanda's back was turned Schewchuck had grabbed her around the neck and throttled her. He'd then clubbed her with a rock, remembering Rev. Dworecki's final words to him, "Strike hard, son."

Dworecki was of course outraged when he was confronted with Peter's confession. But the persistent Dube wore him down too and eventually he broke down and confessed. He hadn't done it for the money, he said, but because of his daughter's promiscuous behavior. He had already been warned that he would be defrocked unless he reined her in.

Dworecki was telling that same story when he came before the courts, but the jury had little sympathy for such a cold-hearted killer, especially one who hid behind a pulpit. They found him guilty and recommended that he should be put to death, a sentence that the judge was happy to deliver.

Walter Dworecki went to the electric chair on March 24, 1940. In a separate trial, Peter Schewchuck, the man who had actually struck the fatal blows was also found guilty. He was sentenced to life in prison.

Robert Keller

Deadly Dancing

Susan Freeman loved to dance. The attractive 34-year-old divorcee could be found just about any night of the week, tripping the night away at some or other nightclub in Melbourne, Victoria. And when she wasn't at a club, she was attending a dance class or providing lessons at the Ace of Clubs dance studio where she worked part-time. It would be safe to say that dancing was an obsession for Susan.

Susan's husband Ian loved dancing too. In fact, it was at a dance competition that he first laid eyes on Susan and was instantly smitten. Ian was married at the time but he and his wife had been living apart for some time. It wasn't long before he'd asked Susan to be his bride and Susan said yes. They tied the knot soon after Ian obtained a divorce in 1987.

The Freemans marriage was by all accounts a happy one, fueled by their mutual love of dancing. Ian was eleven years Susan's senior but he was still a handsome man and an enthusiastic and skilled dance partner. He was also a successful businessman who lavished attention and gifts on his new bride. And Susan was only too happy to accept. Her enthusiasm for shopping ranked second only

to her passion for the dancefloor. She required very little
encouragement to spend her husband's money.

Married bliss continued in this way until 1992 when Ian suffered
an injury and required a knee operation. That of course kept him
sidelined for a while and left Susan frustrated. Not that Ian
discouraged her from going out and enjoying herself. His love of
dancing had in any case waned over the years. He was 50 now and
finding it difficult to keep up with his young wife.

And so Susan began to go out on her own, while Ian stayed home
and spent his evenings with his feet up in front of the television.
Often she'd come home long after he'd retired to bed but if that
bothered Ian, he made no protest. Susan however couldn't help
taunting her husband, calling him an old man and boasting about
the young studs who'd been lining up to take her for a whirl on the
dance floor. Ian said that he was okay with that, as long as she
didn't embarrass him publically. Privately though, he was
beginning to wonder whether it was time to consider ending the
marriage. Stripped of their mutual love of dancing, he and Susan
did not appear to have a whole lot in common.

Enter into this volatile situation a young man named Ian Brown, a
28-year-old fitness fanatic who signed up for dance classes at the
Tattslotto Club in Melbourne in February 1995. Susan was
teaching that class and she was instantly drawn to her latest
student. It wasn't long before she'd made her move and Ian,
perhaps flattered by the attentions of an attractive older woman
responded. Within weeks they were lovers, meeting up at Ian's
apartment after classes for steamy trysts. Soon Susan had begun
complaining to him about her boring stick-in-the-mud husband
and how she wished she could be free of him. Then one night she
stunned Brown by asking if he knew anyone who would kill Ian for
her.

Brown was reluctant at first to have anything to do with Susan's plans. But over the days that followed she gradually wore him down with her tearful outbursts. Ian was making her life a misery she sobbed, draining all the joy out of living. And she couldn't just divorce him because then she'd end up destitute. The only way out, she said, was to have him killed. Failing that, she might have to consider suicide.

It is the oldest trick in the book and one that has been employed by murderous women since time immemorial. And Ian Brown was not the first love-struck young man to fall for it. Eventually he alluded that he might know someone, a man named Max Chatz who worked out at his gym. Chatz (real name: Emmanuel Chatzidimitriou) owned an auto repair shop but often boasted that he made most of his income as a debt collector. He said that he worked for various loan sharks, chasing down tardy debtors and "persuading" them to pay up. And the muscle-bound Chatz was more than interested in the $50,000 Susan Freeman was offering for the hit on her husband. First though he wanted to meet with Susan. Brown set up the meeting and Chatz quickly agreed to take the job. Before long he'd also supplanted Brown in Susan's bed.

The plan that Susan had concocted for the murder of her husband was reliant on two things. First, she wanted it to look like an accident. Second, she had to have a cast iron alibi for the time of the murder. The date that she and Chatz eventually settled on was November 28, 1996. On that day Susan was due to judge a dancing competition and would be seen in public by hundreds of people, the perfect alibi. Ian meanwhile would be going for his usual walk, which his doctor had insisted on to strengthen his knee. Susan knew the route he usually traveled and knew that it took in various remote paths. That would give Chatz the perfect opportunity to abduct him.

Ian Freeman set out for his walk that day never realizing that these would be his last few hours on earth. He had just emerged from a field when Chatz pulled up beside him and jumped from his vehicle holding a gun. Ian knew better than to resist the muscular man who now confronted him, so he got into the car and curled up in the passenger footwell as instructed. Then Chatz drove him to his own house and forced him from the vehicle, again at gunpoint.

The first inkling Ian must have had that Susan was involved was when his abductor produced a set of keys from his pocket and opened the garage door. Ian's hands were then tied and his mouth gagged with duct tape before he was forced roughly into his own vehicle and warned to stay down. Now Chatz got behind the wheel and started driving out of town, eventually stopping at the Cairn Curran reservoir in central Victoria. Once there he got out of the car, released the handbrake and then pushed the vehicle into the water, with Ian still inside.

Unfortunately for Chatz he'd chosen a particularly shallow part of the lake. The car didn't sink as he'd hoped, but hit bottom in less than three feet of water and just sat there. In order to complete the job Chatz had to wade in, pull Ian from the vehicle and force his head under, holding it there until his lungs filled with water and he stopped struggling. Then Chatz removed the gag and rope and fled the scene.

The police first became aware of Ian Freeman's disappearance the following morning when a frantic Susan phoned to report him missing. By then a couple of fishermen had already found Ian's body floating in a reservoir and it did not take the police long to match it to the missing person's report. Called down to the morgue to view the corpse, Susan was quick to provide a theory on what had happened. She said that her husband had been depressed of late and had often spoken of suicide.

That revelation was meant to deflect attention but it did the opposite, elevating Susan to the top of the suspect list. The suicide theory just did not fit the evidence. Drowning is an extremely rare method of taking one's own life. And there were other clues that suggested this was no accident. For starters there were the scratches on Ian's wrist, indicating that he'd probably been tied up. Then there were Ian's glasses. He couldn't drive without them and yet they were not found with his body but lying on the back seat of the car. Finally there were the autopsy results, which revealed tiny hemorrhages behind the victim's eyes. This would not occur in the case of drowning but would be present if the victim had been throttled prior to being shoved under water.

All of the indicators pointed to murder. And who stood to gain most by Ian's death? None other than his widow Susan. The police knew of course that Susan had an alibi for the night of the murder. But they'd never believed that she had killed Ian herself. It was far more likely that she'd hired someone to do her dirty work.

Susan meanwhile was hardly acting like the bereaved widow. Two days after Ian's funeral, she raided the safety deposit box at his bank and removed stamp and coin collections valued at over $25,000. She also hoped no doubt that she'd be generously provided for in his will but here she was in for a surprise. Two weeks before his death, Ian had instructed his attorney to alter the document, disinheriting Susan and leaving the entire estate to his children. Had he perhaps had some suspicion of what his wife was planning? The police had no way of knowing but they firmly believed by now that Susan was involved in her husband's death. Proving it however was another matter.

Fortunately for investigators a surprise witness was about to come forward, providing them with the evidence they needed to solve their case. Ever since reading about Ian Freeman's death in the local papers, Ian Brown had been living in fear of his life. Other than Susan and Chatz, he was the only one who knew the true story behind the murder and that made him vulnerable. Chatz had already proven that he was capable of killing. What was one more murder if it meant getting rid of loose ends? Fearful that he might be killed himself, Brown went to the police and struck a deal – his testimony in exchange for immunity from prosecution.

Ten weeks after Ian Freeman's death, police officers carried out a raid on Max Chatz's home and took him into custody. Then before they could do the same to Susan, she arrived at a police station in the company of her lawyer and handed herself over. Her legal team then got to work on separating her trial from that of Chatz, believing that it offered the best chance of an acquittal.

Susan Freeman appeared before the Victoria Supreme Court in April 1999. By then her co-accused had already been convicted and sentenced to life in prison, but Justice George Hempel ruled in her favor when her attorney filed a petition to have details of that sentence suppressed from the trial. That was a serious setback for the prosecution but they still had a number of cards to play. The evidence of star witness Ian Brown was particularly damning. So too was a letter from Susan to Chatz, which the prison authorities had intercepted. In it she urged him to be strong, to say as little as possible and to accept no deals. "My lips are sealed forever," she concluded, a statement that ironically said more than the spoken word ever could.

On Thursday, May 6, 1999, the jury deliberated for seven hours before returning a guilty verdict against Susan Freeman. The sentence of the court was the same as that handed down to her lover and co-accused – life in prison with a minimum of eighteen years to be served before parole eligibility. Her dancing days, for the next two decades at least were over.

666

Nikolai Ogolobyak

The city of Yaroslavl lies at the confluence of the Volga and the Kotorosl Rivers in western Russia, some 160 miles northeast of Moscow. It is a historic and picturesque burg, surrounded on all sides by dense forest and dotted with wooden Dhakas and those uniquely Russian "onion-bulb" church domes. It is also a world heritage site and home of some of the most stunning examples of Tsarist architecture. Fydor Volkov was born here. So too was Valentina Tereshkova, the first woman in space.

But in June 2008, Yaroslavl achieved a far more dubious celebrity. It was the scene of a quartet of quite horrendous murders, some of the most savage ever committed in the former Soviet state.

To understand the context behind these killings one must first consider the psyche of many Russian citizens during this time. Almost two decades after the fall of the Berlin Wall, many were still struggling with the liberalization of their country. Capitalism may have brought prosperity to the elites but to the average man in the street, life was hard, jobs were few and there was no state support to fall back on. Still, the Russians are a stoic bunch. Most complained about their lot but got on with their lives.

Strangely enough, the group most affected by this socio-political upheaval was one that had no real experience of life under the Soviet regime. Like young people the world over, Russia's youth were naturally rebellious, naturally inquisitive and eager to try new things. Many embraced Western culture, music and fashion; some whole-heartedly pursued the capitalist dream of fame and fortune; still others embraced neo-Nazism or its alter-ego Stalinist Communism. There was also a small but not inconsiderable group who delved into an even darker form of self-expression. In the first decade of the 21st century, there was an explosion of interest in Satanism among the young.

Varya Kuzmina and Andrei Sorokin did not consider themselves devil worshippers. If anything, the teenaged couple were the Russian equivalent of yuppies. Varya, at the age of just 16 had graduated high school a year early and was currently studying towards gaining a license as an insurance broker. Her 18-year-old boyfriend Andrei was an apprentice chef, with dreams of opening his own restaurant someday. The couple however were curious, eager for new experiences. They liked rock music and attending concerts and gigs and it was at one of these that they met 20-year-old Nikolai Ogolobyak.

Ogolobyak was an interesting guy. Dressed all in black and wearing dark eye make-up, he shared Varya and Andrei's interest in rock music and partying. But he had another claim to fame he coyly informed them, he was the high priest of a coven of Satanists. Varya and Andrei at first thought that their new acquaintance was kidding but after establishing that he was dead serious, they began questioning him about it. Where and when did they meet? Did they conjure up demons? Was it true that they sacrificed human babies?

Ogolobyak chuckled at each of those suggestions. "Lies," he assured them. "All lies. All we do is get stoned, listen to Metal and dance naked in the moonlight. We do sometimes read from the Satanic Bible," he added with a wink.

Then a thought appeared to occur to him. "Listen," he said beckoning them closer with a hand gesture. "We're having a gathering tomorrow. Why don't you guys come along and check it out for yourselves?"

Andrei Sorokin left the concert that night with a slip of paper tucked away in his jeans pocket. On it was the address that Ogolobyak had given him but he was by no means certain that he and Varya would take their new friend up on his offer. The guy creeped him out if he was honest about it.

But by the following day curiosity had overcome apprehension. When Andrei phoned Varya late in the afternoon the two agreed that they would attend the "gathering" that they'd been invited to. What was the worst that could happen?

On the evening of Friday, July 18, 2008, a full moon hung ominously over the city of Yaroslavl. The forest clearing to which Andrei and Varya had been summoned however, was all but untouched by its light. Instead the scene was illuminated by a campfire, positioned in the center of the clearing, spitting up sparks and throwing ominous shapes onto the foliage. On one side of the fire Andrei and Varya stood nervously fidgeting, on the other stood their host Ogolobyak along with the rest of his coven. Ogolobyak had already introduced them, using their "worship names" – Klik, Graf, Death, Distress, Corpse and Black Crow. Ogolobyak had a worship name too. His followers called him Dr. Got. They were a strange brood, all of them black-clad with corpselike make-up, dark varnished fingernails and multiple piercings. Now their ranks parted and another of their number was pushed to the fore, an attractive young woman who was entirely naked.

"Friends," Ogolobyak said, addressing his comments to Andrei and Varya. "You are most welcome on this special night. Tonight we initiate Karla into our ranks." Then he placed a hand on the naked girl's shoulder and nodded to one of his followers who went scampering towards a boom box positioned on a tree stump. In the next moment, the forest reverberated with the distorted guitars and guttural grunts of a Death Metal song and the Satanists were dancing around the fire, shaking their heads vigorously and barging into one another in an impromptu mosh pit. One of them handed Varya a beer and another pressed a bottle into Andrei's hand. The gathering it seemed was exactly as Ogolobyak had said it would be.

But then in an instant it all changed. One of the group produced a sack and hauled from its depths a spitting ginger cat. As he held the petrified creature by the tail, another of the group produced a large knife and cut the unfortunate tabby's throat. Varya, who had a similar cat at home squirmed at the sight and cast a worried look towards her boyfriend. He however appeared transfixed by the scene before him. The Satanists were gathering up the slaughtered cat's blood, smearing it on their faces, licking it from their fingers. Then one of them took the animal's corpse and tied it to an upside down cross that had been planted in the earth nearby. It was at that moment that Dr. Got spread his arms and bellowed to his followers. "Seize them!"

Varya and Andrei had been so focused on the gory scene that they'd failed to notice some members of the coven sneaking up behind them. Within moments they were overwhelmed, their hands forced behind their backs, marched towards the center of the circle. Now Dr. Got spoke again, his eyes rolling back in his head as he started reciting an incantation. "Satan, we welcome Karla by offering you these two lives," he intoned. Then one of his followers Graf stepped forward holding the knife, still dripping with the cat's blood. "Do it!" Dr. Got instructed, at which Graf plunged the blade into Andrei's chest.

Andrei Sorokin would suffer a horrendous number of wounds, 666 to be precise, all of them counted out by the Satanists as they passed the knife one to the other and continued stabbing their victim. While they were doing so, Dr. Got periodically stooped and filled his cupped hands with blood which he smeared onto Karla's naked flesh. Then his followers eviscerated Andrei, some of them carrying his excised organs to the fireside where they gorged on the bloody flesh.

It was like a scene from a horror movie, one that was way too gory ever to be shown in a mainstream movie theater. And it was all too much for Varya. Driven almost insane with fear, she collapsed to the forest floor in a dead faint. When she regained consciousness some time later, she found Andrei's murderers gathered in a tight circle around the fire reciting some gibberish verse. They'd left her, temporarily unattended at the edge of the circle.

It was a chance Varya realized, her only chance of getting out of here alive. Summoning every last reserve of courage and strength, she sprang to her feet and went sprinting into the darkness. And she might well have gotten away had she not become disorientated, looped around and run straight back into her pursuers. Then three of them grabbed her, one yanking back her hair while a second hacked through her throat and the third recorded the entire event on his mobile phone.

Nikolai Ogolobyak would not have known this but on the night that he and his satanic followers so brutally murdered Varya Kuzmina and Andrei Sorokin, they were already the subject of a police investigation. Over the previous year, the Yaroslavl police had received a number of complaints regarding "satanic activity." At first these were minor, gravestones were knocked over in local cemeteries, crosses were turned upside down in churches, someone had defecated in a confessional booth. But soon those acts of heresy would escalate. A number of corpses were disinterred and in one particularly grisly case a recently deceased teenaged girl was dug up and hacked to pieces, her body parts distributed to all corners of the graveyard.

Then on July 19, a day before Varya and Andrei were killed, two teenagers Olga Pukhova, 16, and Anya Gorokhova, 15, disappeared. Their parents hadn't initially reported them missing because they thought that the girls had snuck out to attend a rock concert in a neighboring town. Now however the police were faced with four missing person's cases, all of them with a single commonality. Each of the teens had recently befriended a man who their parents described as a "weirdo." That man was Nikolai Ogolobyak.

Ogolobyak was brought in for questioning and it didn't take long for investigators to determine that he was both guilty and certifiably insane. "I have nothing to fear" he raved. "Satan will protect me! I have given him so much blood."

With Ogolobyak in custody the police soon rounded up his followers, a disaffected band of youths aged between 17 and 19, who appeared by daylight to be no more threatening than your average stroppy teenager. They were soon talking, turning on their high priest and claiming that he had threatened and manipulated them into participating in the slaughter. They also led officers to their gathering place in the woods where the mutilated bodies of the four missing teens were found tossed into a pit.

Nikolai Ogolobyak and his group of miscreants were tried before the Yaroslavl Regional Court in July 2010. All but Ogolobyak were found guilty, their prison terms ranging from five to twenty years.

As for the murderous "Dr. Got," he was declared insane and confined indefinitely to a secure psychiatric facility.

Things They Don't Teach You In Sunday School

It is hardly the sort of thing a man wants to hear from his new bride on their wedding night. "I should never have married you. You don't satisfy me sexually." Still, Robert Andrew should have been forewarned. All of his friends had cautioned him about Brenda. She had a reputation. But had that discouraged Rob? Not in the least. From the moment he set eyes on the petite dark-haired beauty going through her paces with the high school cheerleading team, Rob was besotted. Not even a worrying incident during their engagement could deflect him from his path. Rob had been driving past a motel when he'd spotted Brenda coming out of one of the rooms with an ex-boyfriend. He'd later confronted her about it and she'd told him that they'd only gone there to talk. He'd believed her.

And so in 1984 Rob Andrew led his beloved Brenda down the aisle and told everyone who would listen, that he intended spending the rest of his life with her. Over the next ten years they'd have two children Tricity and Parker, and Rob would climb the corporate ladder as an advertising executive while Brenda stayed home to raise the children. To the outside world they looked like the perfect family.

But scratch below the surface and the picture was not quite so rosy. The couple squabbled constantly and it was always Rob who ended up having to make a groveling apology. He was still by all accounts deeply in love with his wife, while she made every effort to rebuff his affections, sometimes embarrassing him in public. In 1993 he convinced Brenda to attend marriage counseling sessions with him, but even that didn't help. It is safe to say that without Rob's determination to hold it together, the marriage would have ended in divorce. That in retrospect would have been a more desirable outcome.

One might well ask why Rob Andrew did not simply walk away from a relationship that was such a source of hurt and frustration to him. Part of the reason was to do with his children and part was to do with his faith. A devout Christian, Rob believed firmly in the 'till death us do part' section of the wedding vows.

But even on matters of faith Brenda was a negative influence. The couple would no sooner establish themselves in a congregation when Brenda would start complaining. She didn't like the pastor or the community looked at them judgmentally or the services were boring. Eventually Rob would give in and they'd move to a new church, only for the whole cycle to begin again. Before long they'd worked their way through just about every Christian church in Oklahoma City.

Then in 1999 came a shift in their relationship. Rob had become involved in the founding of a new congregation, the North Pointe Baptist Church. At first Brenda loved the idea, as it made them one of the most important members of the community. She became actively involved in church affairs and even started teaching Sunday School. But all too soon the veneer of this new life began to wear thin. Rob began to spend more and more time at the church. He stopped drinking and their social life dried up. More to the point, Brenda was losing control over him. Previously she'd bossed and bullied him but now Rob seemed to have a new purpose in life. He was reinvigorated in his faith. For the first time in their relationship, Brenda was relegated to the role of second fiddle. That was never going to be a situation she was prepared to tolerate.

Enter James Pavatt, a deacon at the church and like Brenda a Sunday School teacher. Pavatt had first become acquainted with the Andrews when he sold Rob an $800,000 insurance policy, with Brenda as the sole beneficiary. A man with a somewhat checkered past, Pavatt was going through a divorce when he met Brenda Andrew. It wasn't long before the two of them were involved in a passionate affair.

It is highly unlikely that James Pavatt was the first man with whom Brenda had extramarital relations. Indeed there is evidence to suggest that she was still having casual flings even while she and Pavatt were together. But it was her relationship with Pavatt that caused eyebrows to be raised. The two of them were hardly discreet. They'd sit in church giggling, winking at each other and passing notes like a couple of love-struck teenagers; they'd be seen eating out together at local restaurants; on one occasion, parishioners spotted them making out in Brenda's car in the church parking lot. Eventually Pastor Mark Sinor got tired of all the complaints he was getting from members of his flock and asked James and Brenda to resign their church positions.

Brenda, who saw herself as the wife of the church founder was outraged at the decision, and demanded that Rob either defend her honor or that they quit the church. He however refused. He'd finally found a congregation where he was happy and settled. He was not about to walk away from that. As for defending Brenda's honor, he wondered if there was anything to defend and asked her outright whether there was any truth to the rumors. Was she sleeping with James Pavatt? Brenda strenuously denied that she was.

Over the next ten days an uneasy truce fell over the Andrew household, resolved eventually when Brenda had the locks and the alarm code changed and asked Rob to move out. She then upped the ante by denying him access to his children and refusing to open the door when he came to visit them. Finally, she served him with divorce papers.

That last action was actually a blessing in disguise to Rob. He'd long since given up hope of rescuing his failed marriage and the divorce at least meant that custody issues would be resolved. Even if he did not succeed in gaining guardianship of the children he'd be given visitation rights, rights that Brenda could not legally deny him. Little did he know that Brenda had something altogether more sinister in mind.

On the night of October 25, 2001, just a few days after the divorce papers were served Rob noticed a puddle under his car. Crouching down to inspect the source of the problem, he realized that the liquid was brake fluid and suspected that the lines had been deliberately cut. Rob then phoned the police and reported his suspicion that his estranged wife and her lover were trying to kill him. Detective Mike Kilka responded to the call and confirmed that the damage was deliberate. However there was nothing to link either Brenda or James Pavatt to the sabotage and so no action was taken. Detective Kilka did however warn Rob not to be alone with Brenda and also asked Rob to give him a call should anything else untoward happen.

The following day Rob called James Pavatt and instructed him to change the beneficiary of his life policy from Brenda to the children. Pavatt said that this was not possible since Rob did not own the policy. It was a quite ludicrous assertion and one that Rob quickly put right by phoning the Prudential Insurance Company directly. A couple of days later the company received a document, ostensibly from Rob making Brenda the sole beneficiary again. Since Rob had only recently removed Brenda's name from the policy, a Prudential representative phoned him to verify the new instruction. He of course knew nothing about it. The document authorizing the change would later be proven to be a forgery.

By now you would imagine that Rob Andrew would be extremely wary of his estranged wife. But Brenda still had one hold on him. She still had his children. Rob was desperate to see them so when Brenda unexpectedly phoned him on November 20, 2001, and asked him if he wanted to take them for the Thanksgiving weekend, Rob was delighted. Arrangements were made for him to pick the kids up at 6 p.m. and Rob did not even think to phone Detective Kilka as he'd promised to do. That as it turned out was a tragic mistake.

At around 6:20 that evening, a 911 dispatcher in Oklahoma City received a frantic call. "I've been shot!" the female caller screamed down the line. "My husband and I have been shot!"

Units were immediately dispatched to the scene where they found a man lying face down on the garage floor, dead from two shotgun blasts. The female victim who identified herself as Brenda Andrew, had only a superficial wound to her arm and was taken to the hospital and later discharged. In the interim the police had obtained a statement from her. She said that her husband had been fixing the furnace light in the garage when two masked men had entered. They'd fired twice at her husband with a shotgun and had then shot at her with a handgun before turning and fleeing.

It was a less than convincing story but one that the police had no way of disproving just yet. In the meanwhile, Rob Andrew's grieving family began making funeral arrangements and Brenda

Andrew departed for a vacation in Mexico with her lover and children. Three months later on February 28, 2002, she attempted to return to the US and was nabbed at the border post on a fugitive warrant. She and Pavatt were returned to Oklahoma in cuffs.

Brenda Andrew and James Pavatt would be tried separately for the murder of Rob Andrew. In each case, the prosecution presented a compelling reconstruction of the cold-blooded murder. Rob Andrew had been lured to his death with the promise of a weekend visit with his children. When he'd arrived at the house, Brenda had asked him to check on the pilot light of the furnace which she said was malfunctioning. Rob had crouched down to do that and it was then that James Pavatt had entered, carrying a 16-gauge shotgun. Before Rob could react Pavatt had fired, hitting him in the side.

Rob had staggered to his feet, mortally wounded. Yet he'd still made a vain attempt to protect himself, snatching up a garbage bag filled with empty soda cans as a shield. That had offered scant protection as the second blast had shredded the tin and plastic and ripped through his chest. Based on evidence gleaned from Pavatt, police believed that it was Brenda who'd fired the second shot. She then inflicted a flesh wound on herself with a .22 caliber pistol before calling the police.

James Pavatt was convicted of first-degree murder and sentenced to death in September 2003. Almost a year later in August 2004, Brenda Andrew would hear a judge hand down the same sentence to her. She currently awaits execution.

The Killer Online

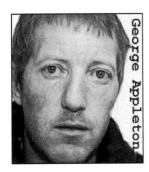

George Appleton

It is every woman's worst nightmare. You meet a handsome stranger who appears to be everything you're looking for in a man, charming, loving and attentive. At first you're wary. After all you hardly know this man. But gradually he wins you over, wins your heart and gets beyond your defenses. You let him into your life and for a time you're glad you did. For a time loneliness has been banished and love blooms. But then things begin to change, small things at first, little flashes of temper, petty jealousies. You let them slide. Perhaps his jealousy even flatters you. And so it escalates, to controlling behavior, to threats of violence, perhaps even to physical abuse. This is when you call time on the relationship. But leaving a man like this is not as easy as saying "it's over." In fact, you've only got him riled. The nightmare has just begun.

This was the terrifying world that Clare Wood inhabited during the last four months of her life. It had all started so innocently. The single mother of one from Salford, Manchester, had been keen to start dating again. At 36, the attractive brunette realized that she wasn't getting any younger. But the idea of finding a male partner to share her life with still appealed to her so when a friend recommended the dating website plentyoffish.com, Clare was keen to give it a try. After posting her profile in April 2007, she was pleasantly surprised to attract a number of potential suitors. The one that most caught her fancy was 40-year-old George Appleton, who described himself in his profile as fun-loving and caring.

But Clare was no fool. She wasn't above to dive headlong into a relationship with a complete stranger. Rather than agree to the date that George asked her on, she suggested that they first get to know each other on Facebook. George appeared to have no problem with that and so they started an online friendship. It wasn't long before he'd begun to win her over with his easy wit and his apparently genial personality. Eventually Clare agreed to meet him in person. A short while later they were an item.

Not everyone was delighted with Clare's choice of partner. Her father Michael (a prison officer and therefore someone with a better than average understanding of miscreants and ne'er-do-goods) disliked Appleton from the start. Clare's brother Adam felt the same way. Both thought that Appleton was hiding something behind that outwardly genial front. But Clare would hear none of it. She described George as "the light of my life." Before long she was talking marriage.

Then on October 2, 2008, a bombshell was dropped on the happy future that Clare Wood had planned with George Appleton. She discovered that throughout their relationship, George had continued to trawl the online dating sites and had in that time been involved with four different women. George of course denied this but the evidence was there for all to see – in his online profile, in his Facebook and e-mail accounts and in his text messages. Clare then ended the relationship. But for the broken heart she'd likely be tending for a while, she considered the affair to be over. For George Appleton however, it was far from over. For him it had only just begun.

To understand a man like Appleton, you must get inside his warped view of the world. Individuals like this are deeply insecure and any rejection only serves to erode the already low opinion that they (subconsciously) hold of themselves. To compensate, they become extremely controlling of those around them. After all, if you control someone then they can never leave you, not unless you say so.

The flipside of this equation is that loss of control sparks panic. If the partner decides to leave anyway, despite the threats and entreaties, that feeling of inadequacy bubbles to the surface and with it comes the almost irresistible impulse to respond. That response can take many forms – crying, threats of suicide or sham suicide attempts, stalking, threats of violence, or actual violence. With a man like George Appleton, it was always going to be the latter. Appleton in fact had a history that would have terrified Clare, had she been aware of it.

In 2002 he'd been jailed for thirty months after a sustained campaign of terror against a former girlfriend. That relationship showed some terrifying parallels to the one that Appleton had with Clare. He'd initially been charming and attentive but after the woman ended the relationship (due to Appleton's infidelity) he began stalking her, harassing her with constant phone calls, threatening violence. On one occasion he threatened to kill her dog, on another he said he was going to throw acid in her face. Eventually, after he told the woman that he was going to burn her alive in her house, she went to the police.

And that was only one example of Appleton's frightening behavior. He'd served a six-month term for similar threats made against another of his ex-girlfriends. He'd kidnapped another at knifepoint. And there were other offences too for which Appleton went unpunished. All of his previous terror campaigns however, would seem trivial compared to what he was about to do to Clare Wood.

On October 7, five days after she ended the relationship, Clare arrived at Pendleton Police Station to report that Appleton had threatened to burn down her house, stab her and beat her to death with an iron bar. Two police officers then escorted her home but no further action was taken. The following day Clare called 999 and advised that Appleton was banging on her door, demanding to be let in. As a result Appleton was arrested, but immediately bailed and warned not to make contact with Clare.

And for a time that warning seemed to have the desired effect. Appleton kept his distance. In the meanwhile, the police advised Clare to have new locks fitted at her home, and gave her details of agencies that assist women suffering domestic violence. They also arranged for a fire assessment to be carried out on her home, in view of Appleton's threat to "burn her alive."

By November, however, Clare appeared to be happy that Appleton no longer posed a threat. So much so in fact, that she wrote a letter to the Greater Manchester Police requesting that Appleton should not be given a custodial sentence at his upcoming trial. She repeated this belief (that Appleton was no longer a threat) during a police visit on December 28. Then she and her ten-year-old daughter traveled to Dewsbury in Yorkshire to spend New Year with her father and brother. During that visit Michael Brown suggested that his daughter move back home, but Clare said that there was no need. Appleton wasn't bothering her anymore.

That truce however did not last long into the new year. On January 18 Clare called the police to report that Appleton had sexually assaulted her. The following day, Appleton contacted police and asked whether Clare had made a complaint. He denied that he'd done anything wrong but was arrested anyway, then immediately bailed. He was again warned not to have any contact with his ex-girlfriend.

Appleton obviously did not understand this instruction because on January 23, Clare reported to the police that he'd sent her several messages via Facebook. Again Appleton was arrested although due to the minor nature of the complaint, he was immediately released.

Now came a twist in the case, one that likely cost Clare Wood her life. On the day of Appleton's latest court appearance, Clare was interviewed on video camera regarding her sexual assault complaint. During that interview she revealed details that she'd not previously shared with the police, details which quite possibly altered the way they viewed the case. Clare admitted under questioning that her contact with Appleton had not been quite as one-sided as she previously stated. She said that she and Appleton had met and spoken on several occasions since the breakup. She also admitted that they'd had consensual sex in November 2008 and that she had gone voluntarily to his apartment on January 17, the day before she'd filed sexual assault charges against him.

Whether or not these revelations had any impact on the outcome of Appleton's next court appearance is unknown. What is known is that the file that was submitted to the Crown Prosecution Services mentioned only criminal damage and omitted any reference to sexual assault. As a result, Appleton was fined for causing malicious damage to Clare's property. He was not issued with a Harassment Notice ordering him to stay away from Clare.

On February 3, Clare's former mother-in-law phoned Michael Brown and told him that she had been trying to raise her on the phone without success. Concerned, Brown then called Clare's ex-husband and asked if he would go to the apartment to check on her. What the unfortunate man found inside would send him running for the phone to call the police. The body lying on the bed was burned and blackened to a crisp and barely recognizable as human. An autopsy would later reveal that Clare Wood had been raped and strangled before her killer poured an accelerant over her body and set her alight. She'd been dead for three days.

There was only ever one suspect for the murder and a nationwide alert was immediately issued for George Appleton. Appleton had lived an itinerant lifestyle, working at fairgrounds all over the country and the police feared that he'd slip the net using his contacts to go underground, or perhaps even to leave the country. They therefore informed all ports and transport networks to be on the lookout.

But George Appleton hadn't gone far. Just a few blocks away to an abandoned pub where he was found six days later. He'd taken his own life by hanging himself from the rafters.

The aftermath of Clare Wood's death had some major implications for British policing and the justice system. An internal investigation concluded that the police had failed to provide adequate protection to a woman whose life was in danger. A campaign was also started by Clare's father Michael Brown, aimed at giving members of the public the ability to run background checks on any individual who they were in a relationship with. This initiative, dubbed Clare's Law came into effect in 2012. Had it been in use when Clare Wood started dating George Appleton, it is likely that she would still be alive today.

Evil is Real

The signs were there for all to see, clues that all was not right and that trouble lay ahead. But such indicators can be subtle and difficult to interpret. How is one to distinguish between the shy, introverted teen and the budding psychopath, head filled with visions of wanton slaughter? One clue might have been the violent child pornography found on Austin Sigg's computer when he was just thirteen years old. That particular indiscretion had earned Sigg a couple of sessions with a psychologist, who had beseeched the boy's father to restrict his son's internet access. Whether that advice was ever heeded is uncertain.

Fast-forward four years to 2012 and we find Austin Sigg enrolled in the forensic science program at Arapahoe Community College in Littleton, Colorado. The obviously intelligent teen had quit school the previous year, driven out by bullies who constantly picked on him because of his high-pitched voice. A high school equivalency test had seen him admitted to college but even here he remained isolated from his classmates. They found him "weird," "frighteningly intense" and "obsessed with death." While most of the forensics students hoped for a career in law enforcement, Austin informed them that he planned on becoming a mortician.

But perhaps there was another reason for Austin Sigg's choice of major, perhaps he thought that a knowledge of police detection techniques would be useful to him in the secondary career he was planning. Austin you see had never outgrown his childhood fascination with sexual violence. Like most budding psychopaths, he'd spent years nurturing the violent images that circulated in his brain. In his case, those visions centered not on aberrant sex or the act of murder. His particular predilection was for dissection. The thought of having a human body to carve apart and examine instilled in him a feeling of sexual arousal that was almost too intense to bear. Eventually, it drove him to action.

On the morning of Monday, May 28, 2012, Sigg got into his Jeep Cherokee and drove to Ketner Lake, near his home in Westminster, Colorado. Concealed within his pocket was a bottle of chloroform which he'd cooked up using a recipe he'd found on the internet. His plan was cursory at best. He was going to conceal himself in bushes beside some isolated path and wait for a lone female to pass by. He'd then come up behind her and clamp a chloroform-soaked rag over her face. After she passed out, he'd drag her into the bushes and rape her. He might even strangle her to death and then cut her. He hadn't decided on that part yet.

Sigg didn't have to wait long for a potential victim to appear. He'd barely crouched down in the brush when he spotted a female jogger coming up the path towards him. Steadying his nerves with a couple of deep breaths, he waited until she passed and then broke cover with his chloroform cloth in hand. The woman however must have heard him because she turned just as he was about to grab her. A brief struggle then ensued before the potential victim broke free and sprinted away. She later reported the incident to the police. By the time they arrived, Austin Sigg was long gone.

Sigg was frustrated but not discouraged by his failure. He realized now that he'd made a crucial mistake in targeting a victim who was strong enough to fight back. What he needed was someone who was easy to overpower. He'd always had a preference for children anyway.

Jessica Ridgeway was a joy to all who knew her. The fifth-grader was a bundle of energy with a mischievous sense of humor and a genuinely caring nature. She loved the color purple and performing in a peewee cheerleading squad at Witt Elementary. She was on her way to that school on October 5, 2012, when she disappeared.

At around 10 a.m. that morning, a school administrator placed a courtesy call to Jessica's mother, wanting to find out if Jessica was okay. Sarah Ridgeway however did not get the call as she was asleep, having just returned home from working a night shift. It was only at 4:30 p.m. that she picked up her voicemail and learned that her daughter was missing. She immediately called the Westminster police but it would be five hours before all of the criteria was met to issue an Amber Alert.

By then a massive search was already underway, one that would eventually involve over 1,000 police and civilian volunteers. But as the days passed with no sign of the missing girl, hopes of finding her alive began to appear more and more remote. And the optimism of investigators was not improved when Jessica's backpack was found on a sidewalk in Superior, over six miles from her home. That discovery seemed to indicate that Jessica had been abducted. The backpack did however provide the Colorado Bureau of Investigation with a piece of evidence that could be checked for trace DNA. They'd only just sent the bag off for processing when they got the news everyone had been dreading.

Late on the afternoon of October 11, two municipal workers discovered a heavy garbage bag near Pattridge Park Open Space in Arvada. One of the men split the bag open with his pocket knife and shook its contents out onto the ground. Moments later the two men reeled back in horror. The bag contained the dissected torso of a child.

Jessica Ridgeway had been found but her killer was still out there and a ripple of fear ran through the community. What kind of a monster would murder and mutilate an innocent little girl and how long before he targeted another child? As concerned parents began escorting their children to and from class, officers guarded crosswalks and photographed cars parked outside schools. Meanwhile Westminster took on a mantle of purple as residents adorned their mailboxes in ribbons, to honor Jessica. At around that time the police also issued a public appeal, urging citizens to come forward with any information, no matter how trivial. On October 19, one of them heeded the call.

The caller did not have anything tangible to share. All he would say was that the police should talk to Austin Sigg, a local teen who the informant insisted was "obsessed with death." On the face of it that did not seem like a very promising lead, but the police were desperate for a break in the case and so two CBI agents visited Sigg's residence that same afternoon. The youngster was entirely co-operative, answering questions and agreeing to provide DNA for testing. By the time the agents left with DNA samples in hand, they were convinced that they'd been sent on a fool's errand.

But the case was about to take a dramatic turn. On October 23, before the results of Sigg's DNA test were in, a 911 dispatcher in Jefferson County received a most unusual call. The caller identified herself as Mindy Sigg. This is the actual transcript.

Mindy Sigg: "Hi, um, I need you to come to my house ... um, my son wants to turn himself in for the Jessica Ridgeway murder."

Dispatcher: "And what's going on there. Ma'am, are you there?"

Mindy Sigg: "Did you not hear me? He just confessed to killing her."

Dispatcher: "I know. I want you to tell me what's going on. Can you tell me exactly what he said?"

Mindy Sigg: "That he did it and gave me details and her remains are in my house."

The dispatcher then asked if she could speak to Austin directly.

Austin Sigg: "I don't exactly get why you're asking me these questions. I murdered Jessica Ridgeway."

Dispatcher: "Okay."

Austin Sigg: "There is ... I have proof that I did it ... there is no other question. You just have to send a squad car down here."

The squad car had, in fact, already been dispatched. When the officers arrived Sigg was true to his word. He gave himself up without offering any resistance. As a juvenile, he was taken to the Mount View Services Center and it was there that detectives began interrogating him. He seemed almost keen to tell his story.

Asked why he'd chosen Jessica, Sigg simply shrugged and said that she was at the "wrong place, wrong time." "I was just driving and just kind of looking," he said. "And I saw her. And I parked, and I waited. And she walked by, and I grabbed her."

He said that he'd pulled her into the back seat of his car and had secured her arms and legs with zip ties. He'd then driven around for a while before taking her back to his house. There he told her to change into some clothes he had picked out for her. Then he put on a movie for her to watch while he cut her hair. Finally he tried to strangle her, using a zip tie. When that cut into his hands and failed to provide the right amount of leverage, he resorted to manual strangulation, throttling her for about three minutes until she blacked out.

But Jessica was still not dead and as she lay twitching on the floor, Sigg dragged her to the bathroom, filled the tub with scalding hot water and drowned her in it. He then began dissecting the corpse in the bath, neatly wrapping and labeling the body parts. Some of these he'd later discard. Others, like the head and vagina he'd keep hidden in the crawlspace beneath the house.

Asked why he had dismembered the body, Sigg said that he was fulfilling a sexual fantasy. However, he emphatically denied sexually assaulting the ten-year-old. This, the medical examiner would determine was a lie. Jessica had indeed been raped.

And so Austin Sigg was brought before the Jefferson County District Court in October 2013. Against the advice of counsel he entered guilty pleas to all of the charges, secure in the knowledge that his age at the time of the murder precluded him from the death penalty. In fact the mandated sentence for someone of his age was life in prison, with parole eligibility after 40 years. Judge Stephen Munsinger however, was determined that Sigg should spend the rest of his days behind bars. He sentenced Sigg to an additional 86 years, to run consecutively with his life sentence. That means that if Sigg ever earns parole, he will immediately have to begin serving the 86-year term. It is unlikely that he will ever walk the streets again.

That of course is of scant consolation to Jessica Ridgeway's grieving family. A monster entered their lives in October 2012, cruelly snatching away a precious little girl for no other reason than to satisfy his perverted needs. To quote a line from Judge Munsinger's closing statement: "Evil is real. It was present in our community on October 5, 2012. On that day, its name was Austin Sigg."

The Hamilton Torso Murder

Evelyn Dick

On the afternoon of Saturday, March 16, 1946, a group of children were playing on the Niagara Escarpment, outside the town of Hamilton in Ontario, Canada. The area, known locally as The Mountain is heavily wooded, so when one of the boys spotted a pinkish object protruding from the undergrowth, he was uncertain what it was. On closer inspection the children decided that it was the gutted carcass of a pig. Nonetheless the kids reported the find to their parents. That was how word eventually reached the local police and a couple of constables were given the task of investigating. What they found would launch one of the most sensational murder cases in Canadian history.

The carcass as it turned out, did not belong to a pig but to an adult human male. His arms, legs and head had been removed but wounds to the torso indicated that he'd been shot before being dismembered. A deep cut across the abdomen also suggested that the killer had tried to saw the torso in half but had abandoned that effort. But who was the victim? A scan of recent missing persons' reports turned up one likely candidate, a streetcar conductor by the name of John Dick, who had been reported missing by his cousin Alexander Kammerer on March 6. Kammerer was asked to come down and view the remains and immediately identified Dick by a scar on his side.

With the victim now identified, investigators set about finding his killer. The obvious place to start was with John Dick's estranged wife Evelyn. She as it turned out, had a somewhat scandalous reputation in Hamilton. Her response to news of her husband's death was also interesting. "Don't look at me" she snapped back at the officers delivering the tragic news. "I don't know anything about it."

Evelyn Dick (nee: MacLean) was born in Beamsville, Ontario on October 13, 1920. A year after her birth her parents Donald and Alexandra moved the family to Hamilton, where Donald found work as a conductor on the Hamilton Street Railway. The family however had aspirations of a much higher social status than that, and it appears that they regarded their daughter as a meal ticket to greater things. From an early age it was clear that Evelyn was going to grow into a rare beauty. Dark-haired and dark-eyed with an engaging smile, she captivated all who met her. It was also apparent early on that the child was not well-developed mentally.

The McLeans were highly protective of their daughter, prohibiting her from having friends and keeping her indoors a great deal of the time, claiming that she was too fragile to engage in the normal rough and tumble play of children. But behind the doors of the family home at 214 Rosslyn Avenue, Evelyn had no such protection. Donald McLean was a heavy drinker and he and his wife fought often and regularly. Aside from that, there is evidence to suggest that Donald sexually molested his daughter.

There were rumors too that Donald was dipping into the coffers of his employers. By now he'd progressed from riding the rails to riding a desk, processing the company's daily receipts. And some of that money undoubtedly found its way into his pockets. How else could you explain the McLeans' lavish lifestyle? Evelyn, by now a precocious mid-teen, dressed only in the finest couture and wore jewels and furs that definitely exceeded her father's rate of pay. The McLeans also hosted lavish parties at Hamilton's plush Royal Connaught Hotel. The idea was to introduce Evelyn to the city's social elite but in that respect it failed dismally. The moneyed classes were quite happy to quaff free champagne but they were less inclined to welcome a tram conductor's daughter into their ranks.

The Royal Connaught parties did however introduce Evelyn to one sector of the elite who were more than happy to keep company with her. She was seen around town with a number of wealthy older men, most of them married. When she became pregnant in 1942 the rumor mill went into overdrive, speculating as to the identity of the father. Evelyn quashed these by insisting that she'd secretly married a serviceman named White, who had since been shipped overseas. She even christened her child, a daughter born October 1942 with the name Heather White. Heather unfortunately was born with severe mental retardation.

The following year and with Evelyn's mysterious husband still absent, she was pregnant again, although the baby was stillborn. Then on September 5, 1944, she gave birth to a son Peter David White. No one is certain of who the father of these children was, although it has been suggested that Heather's retardation points to an incestuous union.

Whether that is true or not, Evelyn was soon to remove herself from her father's direct influence. In June of 1945, she and her mother left Donald behind and moved into an apartment in downtown Hamilton. About a month later Evelyn announced to her mother that she was engaged to be married, with the wedding planned for two weeks hence. Alexandra was initially delighted, certain that her daughter had at last snagged one of her wealthy beaus. Imagine her shock when Evelyn revealed the identity of her fiancée. His name was John Dick and like Donald McLean, he worked as a conductor on the Hamilton Street Railway.

How exactly a nobody like Dick had managed to woo a beauty like Evelyn is not known. But Evelyn had always been prone to impulsive decision making, a consequence of her less than stellar mental capacities. A psychiatrist who later examined her would put her mental age at thirteen. The marriage to John Dick at any rate got off to a bad start. When Dick proudly took his new bride to an apartment he'd leased for them on Barton Street, Evelyn tartly informed him, "You must be crazy if you think I'm going to live in that flophouse."

Instead she continued to live with her mother, informing Dick that he couldn't move in as there wasn't enough room for him. This strange arrangement continued for the first month of the Dicks' marriage until Evelyn put down a deposit on a two-story house at 32 Carrick Avenue. In the meanwhile she continued to sleep with a former lover named Bill Bohozuk.

After the purchase of the Carrick Street property, Mr. and Mrs. Dick finally set up home together. But relations between them were far from cordial. They fought and bickered constantly, leading to John's departure from the house on March 6, 1946. The next time anyone saw him was when his dismembered corpse turned up on the Niagara Embankment. Now his less-than-bereaved widow was denying any involvement in his murder.

That is not to say that Evelyn was without a theory as to what had happened to her husband. She offered investigators a bizarre story about a nattily dressed "Italian-looking guy" who had arrived at her door looking for John. According to Evelyn, the man had said he was going to "fix" John for messing around with his wife.

The investigators gave very little credence to that quite ludicrous tale. In fact, it caused them to focus their attention more intently on Evelyn. They went looking for clues that might link her to the murder and a few days later they had one. A man named Bill Landeg reported that he'd lent his Packard sedan to Evelyn and that the car had been returned with bloodstains on the front seat and items of bloody clothing in the trunk. Evelyn had apologized for the mess claiming that Heather had cut herself. However, when police tested the blood they found that it matched John Dick's type.

Confronted with this evidence, Evelyn concocted a new story, this one even more ridiculous than her first. She now said that she had received a call from a mysterious man who'd told her that John had made a woman pregnant and that he had "got what was coming to him." The man had instructed her to borrow a car and to meet with him. Evelyn had done so, arriving to find the man holding a large sack. He told her it contained "a part of John" and instructed her to drive to the Niagara Embankment, where he dumped the remains. Asked why she'd gone along with the man and hadn't reported the incident to the police, Evelyn said that John had pulled a "pretty mean trick" by impregnating a married woman and "breaking up a home." He had got what he deserved. However, she denied having anything to do with John's murder or of conspiring to kill him. Later Evelyn changed her version of events again, returning to the Italian hitman story. Only this time the hitman had been hired by her lover Bill Bohozuk.

None of these stories came even close to convincing investigators of Evelyn's innocence. Instead they got to work gathering evidence to prove her guilt, beginning with a search of the Carrick Avenue residence. There they hoped to find evidence of murder, blood spatters, bloody clothing, perhaps the murder weapon itself. What they uncovered instead was another murder. Inside a large suitcase in the attic were the dismembered remains of an infant boy, later identified as Evelyn's son Peter David White.

So who had killed baby Peter? Alexandra MacLean was quick with an answer. She said it was her estranged husband Donald. According to Alexandra, she'd seen Donald haul the case up to the attic. When she'd asked him about it, he'd told her to "mind her own damn business." As for Evelyn, when she was asked about her son's murder she came up with yet another story. This one however was easier to believe. She now said that Bill Bohozuk had murdered both John Dick and the child.

Warrants were duly issued for Bohozuk and Donald McLean and a search of McLean's basement soon unearthed a wealth of incriminating evidence. There was a loaded revolver, ammunition, a couple of bloodstained saws and a pair of bloody shoes that was identified as belonging to John Dick. Evelyn Dick, Bill Bohozuk and Donald MacLean were then charged with murder.

The three defendants would be tried separately but it was Evelyn's trial that attracted the most attention. The case in fact was a media sensation, with the national press dissecting, analyzing and regurgitating every lurid detail. At the Main Street courthouse crowds gathered every day, jostling for a seat to the greatest show in town, the shocking tale of Hamilton's own 'Black Widow.'

And Evelyn didn't disappoint. One particular exchange with the prosecutor aptly illustrates the sensationalist nature of the testimony.

"Isn't it true," the lawyer asked, "that the father of your child could have been any one of 400 men in this city?"

"No, not that many," Evelyn replied.

"Three hundred, then," he suggested.

"Well, no."

"Tell the court then, how many men you've had sexual intercourse with," the lawyer demanded.

"Maybe 150," Evelyn said, to much titillation from the gallery.

"Mrs. Dick," said the lawyer, "I want you to name these men for the court right now. Who are they?"

"Well, his son for one," Evelyn replied.

"Were you indicating his honor?" the lawyer asked, incredulously.

"Yes, the judge's son," Evelyn said, at which point the judge stepped in and disallowed the line of questioning.

Titillation and scandal aside, there was plenty of evidence linking Evelyn Dick to the murders of her husband and son. No one was suggesting that she'd pulled the trigger herself or that she'd personally hacked the corpse apart, but there could be no denying that she was involved in the conspiracy and was at the very least, party to the disposal. As such, it was no surprise when after nine days of testimony the jury returned a guilty verdict. That of course carried the sentence of death by hanging.

But Evelyn would never make the short walk to the gallows. Her attorney, J.J. Robinette appealed the sentence and was successful in having it overturned, on the grounds that Evelyn's statements to police were improperly admitted into evidence and that the trial judge had not properly instructed the jury.

Evelyn was released from custody only to be immediately rearrested and charged with killing her son. The charge this time was manslaughter and the subsequent conviction earned her a life sentence. In the interim Bill Bohozuk had walked on his murder rap after Evelyn refused to testify against him at trial. And Donald MacLean had been found guilty as an accessory to murder and sentenced to five years in prison.

Evelyn Dick would serve only eleven years of her life sentence before being paroled in 1958. Thereafter she was given a new identity and promptly disappeared from public life. No one knows for certain what happened to her, although there are unverified rumors that she married a wealthy man and lived out the rest of her days in obscurity on Canada's west coast.

Killing Mary

Mary Henderson Morris was a woman of regular habits. The 48-year-old financial advisor had a job at Chase Manhattan bank in Spring Valley, Houston where she was a diligent, well-liked and reliable employee. So when Mary failed to show up for work on October 12, 2000, her colleagues were immediately concerned. And a call to Mary's husband only increased the level of anxiety. According to Jay Morris, his wife had left for work at 6 a.m. as she always did. After placing calls to friends and relatives, all of whom had neither seen nor heard from Mary, Jay called the police.

Then, at around 5 p.m. that afternoon, came the call that Mary's family had been dreading. A burned out Chevy Lumina, similar to the one that Mary drove had been found in a remote area of Harris County, the driver still at the wheel but burned beyond recognition. The official identification would be a while in coming. Mary Morris was so thoroughly incinerated that the only way to identify her was by her teeth.

As friends and family of the deceased tried to come to terms with this tragic and wholly unexpected death, the question that kept popping up was why. Who on earth would have wanted to harm such a thoroughly nice woman? Mary had no known enemies, was blissfully happy in her marriage and was both well-liked and well-respected at her place of work. Robbery was briefly considered as a motive but just as quickly dismissed. Mary's wedding ring and purse were missing from the scene but the pair of diamond earrings she'd been wearing was found among the ashes. The police also could not understand why a thief would have gone to such extreme lengths to get rid of the body, driving the car out into the middle of nowhere and then pouring on an accelerant and torching it with the victim inside. It just didn't make sense.

Investigators were still mulling over that question when they got a bizarre lead in the case. On October 13, a day after Mary's death, someone called a reporter at the Houston Chronicle and uttered a single, cryptic sentence. "They got the wrong Mary Morris," he said before hanging up.

The tip was duly passed on to Houston PD and almost immediately dismissed as a hoax. The information after all seemed nonsensical. The wrong Mary Morris? What was that supposed to mean? Three days later the police had their answer when another woman was murdered. Like Mary Henderson Morris this woman was found dead in her car. This time however there'd been no fire to destroy evidence, so it was easy to determine cause of death. The woman had been beaten and then shot in the head. But what was really astounding was the victim's name – Mary McGinnis Morris.

Two women named Mary Morris had now been slain, their deaths separated by three days and only a few miles. The odds of that happening, surely, were phenomenal. And given the tip-off that the mystery caller had phoned in to the Chronicle, surely the crimes must be connected? "They got the wrong Mary Morris," the caller had said. Did that mean that someone had put out a hit on Mary McGinnis Morris and a bumbling hitman had murdered Mary Henderson Morris before realizing his mistake and putting matters right?

On the face of it that appeared to be a compelling explanation. The two women bore a passing resemblance to one another, were of a similar age and drove similar cars. Plus of course, they shared a name. Moreover, while Mary Henderson Morris was bereft of enemies, there were at least two men who might have wanted Mary McGinnis Morris dead.

A recent arrival in Texas from her native West Virginia, McGinnis Morris' 17-year marriage was on the rocks, due to an accusation that she'd been having an affair with a family friend. And there were financial strains on the relationship too. Mary's husband Mike had been unable to find work in Houston and had been effectively unemployed since their move from West Virginia. Then there was the sizeable insurance policy on Mary's life with Mike as sole beneficiary. Might that have been a motive for murder? Detectives knew that in cases of spousal homicide, it often was.

Mike Morris however was not the only suspect. Mary had trouble at work too. A qualified nurse, she had come to Houston to take up the position of medical director at chemicals giant Union Carbide. She was good at her job and generally well-liked but early in 2000, the company had employed a male nurse named Duane Young and he and Mary had immediately found themselves at loggerheads. Several clashes followed with matters coming to a head on the Friday before Mary was killed. On that day, Mary had arrived at work to find the words "Death to Her" scrawled on her desktop calendar. She'd reported the incident and the subsequent inquiry had led to Duane Young being fired. Thereafter Mary was apparently so afraid of Young seeking revenge, that she had asked her husband to buy her a gun for protection.

That weapon had been tucked safely under the driver's seat of Mary's vehicle as she drove into work on Sunday, October 15. Mary was not on duty that day, but she'd come into the office to administer a flu shot to her friend and co-worker Laurie Gemmell. A short while after they parted company, Mary called Gemmell and told her that she was doing some shopping and had spotted someone who was "giving her the creeps." She didn't name names but Gemmell got the impression it might be Duane Young or an associate of his. Yet Mary didn't seem unduly concerned. Her tone according to Laurie Gemmell's later statement was "matter of fact."

But the call that Mary made twelve minutes after ending her conversation with Laurie Gemmell was anything but matter of fact. It was placed to a 911 dispatcher and while no transcript has ever been made public, it is widely believed that it captured Mary Morris' last moments on earth. Certainly the police hinted at that when they described the call as "chilling, very disturbing."

Mary McGinnis Morris' Dodge Intrepid was found on West Little York Street the following day, less than 25 miles from the secluded woodland where Mary Henderson Morris' car had been incinerated four days earlier. The vehicle's passenger-side door was open and the corpse of Mary Morris lay inside, a single gunshot wound to the temple. That however was not the only injury. The victim had been badly beaten and defensive wounds on her arms indicated that she'd fought valiantly for her life. Yet inexplicably the killer had tried to stage the death as a suicide. Mary had been shot with her own gun, the same weapon she'd apparently begged her husband to buy for her, a weapon that was registered in his name.

And there was soon other evidence that caused the police to elevate Mike Morris to the head of their suspect list. Phone records revealed a call, four minutes in duration, that was made to Mary's phone two hours after her frantic 911 call. The caller was none other than Mike Morris and the police wanted to know who he'd been talking to, since Mary was dead by that time. Confronted with that question, Mike admitted that he'd made the call but insisted that it had gone unanswered. He'd allowed it to ring, he said, because he was desperately trying to contact his wife. That of course was an impossibility; the phone company's logs indicated that the phone had definitely been answered. But Mike stuck to his guns and then refused to answer any further questions without having a lawyer present.

Mike Morris was free to go but the police continued to pursue him as their main suspect. He had motive and opportunity, he had knowledge of where the murder weapon was stashed, he stood to gain financially by his wife's death. And then there was another piece of circumstantial evidence tying him to the murder. A few months after Mary's death, a ring that had been reported missing from the crime scene magically reappeared – on the finger of Mike Morris' daughter from a previous relationship. Questioned regarding this discrepancy, Morris claimed that he'd found the ring at home after his wife's murder and had forgotten to inform detectives.

That oversight seems highly suspicious given that the missing ring was assumed to have been carried from the crime scene by Mary's killer. But despite the best efforts of detectives, there simply was not enough evidence to charge Mike Morris with murder. Eventually the McGinnis Morris case, like that of Mary Henderson Morris went cold. The murders remain unsolved to this day and so too does the central mystery surrounding the cases. Were the killings of the two Mary's connected and if so, how? Alternatively, was it all just a massive coincidence?

The odds of two women with the same name being murdered in the same city within three days of each other have been calculated at a staggering 46 million to one. Add to that the fact that the women resembled one another, drove similar cars and were both murdered in their vehicles and the figure becomes more astronomical still. What then was the connection between the murders?

Perhaps the best clue comes from the mysterious phone call made to the Houston Chronicle in the aftermath of Mary Henderson Morris' murder. "They got the wrong Mary Morris," the caller had said, suggesting that some other woman named Mary Morris was the target. That woman undoubtedly was Mary McGinnis Morris, who was killed just days later. And that in turn seems to support the bumbling hitman theory.

And yet the Houston PD were unconvinced at the time and continues to reject the possibility of mistaken identity. Instead, they offer an alternate explanation – that while plotting to kill Mary McGinnis Morris, her killer learned of the fortuitously timed murder of Mary Henderson Morris and decided to use it as a way of deflecting attention from himself. That explanation, to me at least, feels far less compelling. Chances are that we will never know the answer.

A Twist in the Plot

Arthur Upfield had come to Australia to start a new life. The Englishman, born in Gosport, Hampshire on September 1, 1890, had originally planned on earning his living as a real estate agent but had done poorly in the entrance exams for his chosen profession. Then after the outbreak of World War I, he enlisted in the Australian Imperial Army and was posted to Egypt. He later fought at Gallipoli and in France, where he met an Australian nurse who would become his wife. After the cessation of hostilities he returned to Australia and over the next 20 years he lived a somewhat nomadic lifestyle, traveling throughout the outback and working at a number of low-skilled jobs.

In1929, Upfield was employed as a boundary rider, patrolling the Rabbit-Proof Fence. This 2,000-mile stretch of wire had been erected to keep grazing wildlife away from Western Australia's agricultural heartland. But the rugged terrain that it covered meant that the fence needed constant maintenance. This repair work required riders to patrol allotted sections of the fence, detecting and repairing gaps. It was tough solitary work but it suited Upfield perfectly. The solitude gave him the perfect opportunity to work on his secondary career. By then he'd already published three detective novels and was working on a fourth.

The hero of Upfield's books was a mixed-race sleuth by the name of Detective Inspector Napoleon Bonaparte, or Bony for short. The son of a Caucasian father and an Aboriginal mother, Bony used ancient Aboriginal wisdom and modern forensic techniques to solve various crimes, often while working undercover as a farmhand. The series would ultimately run to 37 novels and would become wildly popular in Australia and beyond. At the time that our story takes place however, Upfield had met with scant success. He hoped that his fourth offering, tentatively titled 'The Sands of Windee' would change that.

Upfield had a problem though. He wanted to make this Bony's toughest case yet, a murder that would be virtually impossible to solve. Unable to come up with an idea that was devious enough, he threw the problem out to his fellow riders around the campfire one night. How would one dispose of a body so that it would never be found?

One of those present, a man named George Ritchie had an idea. He'd kill his victim with strychnine, he said, since it was used to poison dingoes and was thus readily available. Then he'd burn the body, along with the carcass of a large kangaroo to camouflage any bone fragments that might remain. He'd then sift through the bones to remove metal fragments like tooth fillings. These would be dissolved in acid, once again, easily obtained since it was used in mining operations in the area. The bones meanwhile would be pounded and ground to dust and then tossed to the four winds. No one would ever find the slightest trace of a body that had been disposed of in that way.

Upfield agreed that this was indeed an excellent disposal method. But it created a new problem. In any good detective novel, the villain has to slip up in some small way, leaving behind some miniscule clue for the fictional detective to latch onto. What, Upfield wanted to know, might be the flaw in Ritchie's method?

Over the hours that followed the two men batted the problem back and forth, with their fellow riders chipping in here and there to offer ideas and suggestions. By the time they all retired to their bedrolls, the problem was still up in the air and the following day it still remained unresolved. Eventually Upfield issued a challenge to his colleagues, offering a bounty of £1 to anyone who could find a chink in the otherwise perfect plan. That prize had still not been claimed by October 1929, when a man named Snowy Rowles got to hear of it.

Rowles was not a boundary rider like Upfield and Ritchie but worked as a stockman on local farms and was known as a skilled bush tracker. He was a handsome and amiable man who was well liked in the area. What his employers and acquaintances did not know however was that he was a fugitive from justice. His real name was John Thomas Smith and in July 1928 he'd been arrested for robbing a general store in Dalwallinu, Western Australia. Thereafter he'd overpowered a police officer and escaped from the Dalwallinu lock-up. He'd shown up later in the Murchison area where he began looking for laboring jobs, using the name Rowles. Now he listened intently as the possible solutions to Upfield's "perfect murder" were floated, batted around and then rejected.

On December 8, 1929, Snowy Rowles was drinking at a bar in the town of Burracoppin, in Western Australia's "Wheat Belt," when he struck up a conversation with two men, James Ryan and George Lloyd. Ryan was the fencing contractor responsible for Rabbit-Proof Fence No. 1, a span of wire that terminated just outside of Burracoppin. It was his habit to come into town once a month to deposit his check and pick up supplies. After that he'd usually retire to the bar and get falling down drunk. Often he'd leave town passed out in the bed of his truck, with one of his employees at the wheel. The employee allocated to the job of driver this month was the strictly teetotal George Lloyd. When Rowles asked if he could hitch a ride with them, Lloyd was happy to oblige. He said he'd be glad of the company.

James Ryan and George Lloyd were never seen alive again after that day and although there was some talk about their sudden disappearance, it went no further than that. Fence riders were an itinerant lot who often upped sticks and left the area without informing anyone. Why exactly James Ryan would have walked away from a lucrative fencing contract appears not to have been widely discussed. Nor was anyone particularly perturbed when Snowy Rowles was spotted driving Ryan's truck. Rowles was careful to avoid Burracoppin, where Ryan was well-known and where questions might well have been asked. To everyone else he told conflicting versions of how he'd come into possession of the vehicle. Sometimes he said that Ryan had lent it to him. On other occasions he raised eyebrows by insisting that he'd bought it. Everyone knew that Snowy Rowles was flat broke. Still, no one thought to mention these inconsistencies to the authorities.

Five months later in May 1930, Rowles was in Wydgee Station when he started chatting to a New Zealander named Louis Carron. Carron had recently arrived in the area and had been working on a nearby farm. He was spotted on that day heading out of town with Rowles and was never seen alive again. The following day Louis Carron's paycheck was cashed in the neighboring town of Paynesville, and a couple of kangaroo hunters spotted Snowy Rowles tending a large fire near the Rabbit-Proof Fence. The men thought nothing of it and went on their way when Rowles told them that he was "just having a cleanup."

But Rowles had miscalculated in his choice of victim this time. Carron had friends and family and he kept in regular contact with them. When they suddenly stopped hearing from him, they contacted the authorities and asked them to look into his disappearance.

Detective Sergeant Harry Manning was assigned to the case and it did not take long before the pieces of the puzzle started slotting into place. Rowles had hardly been discreet. He'd been seen leaving Wydgee Station with Carron and as Manning now learned, had also been keeping company with two other men – Ryan and Lloyd – just before they went missing. Moreover he was now driving one of the missing men's truck, and had also been flush with money the day after Louis Carron's paycheck was cashed at the Paynesville bank. The clincher came when the kangaroo hunters reported that they'd seen Rowles burning something near the fence and led the police to the exact spot. There they found the remains of Louis Carron's body – several shards of bone, a number of teeth and perhaps most importantly, a unique wedding ring.

Carron as it turned out had been living under an alias, just like his killer. His real name was Leslie George Brown and he had a wife back in New Zealand. She reported that the ring was unique because a jeweler had used the wrong grade of gold when re-sizing it. As a result there was a thin strip that was a slightly different color. The ring now in Detective Manning's possession certainly matched that description. And there was further confirmation when Manning tracked down a dentist in Perth who had done work on the victim's teeth and was able to identify that work from photographs of the remains.

Snowy Rowles a.k.a. John Thomas Smith was arrested for murder in May 1930. Since the remains of James Ryan and George Lloyd had never been found he was charged only for the murder of Louis Carron. Detective Manning however was in no doubt that he was responsible for all three deaths. He believed that Rowles had followed Arthur Upfield's fictional murder plot to the letter when getting rid of Ryan and Lloyd but had become careless when disposing of Louis Carron. As to the method of murder, the state of the body made that impossible to determine. It is likely that

Rowles shot his victims, although he may well have poisoned them, as suggested in the story idea.

Despite the circumstantial nature of the evidence, there was very little chance that Snowy Rowles would escape justice, especially after Arthur Upfield was called to the stand. Upfield's testimony left the jury in no doubt that Rowles was aware of the body disposal method mooted for Upfield's upcoming book. Had he been more diligent in applying the method, he might well have escaped the noose.

Snowy Rowles was hanged at Perth on June 13, 1931.

FOOTNOTE: The publicity generated by the murder trial made Arthur Upfield's fourth novel 'The Sands of Windee' a bestseller. He would go on to both commercial and critical success. But it is said that the murders haunted him for the rest of his life and that he considered them too much of a price to pay for the fame he ultimately achieved. Arthur Upfield died in 1964.

For My Sister

We've all read or heard about the unique bond that exists between identical twins. The siblings do not only resemble one another, they tend to adopt each other's mannerisms, to complete each other's sentences. Sometimes, they even seemed to be able to anticipate each other's thoughts.

That was certainly the case with Teresa and Lisa Seabolt. The twins had been born within an hour of one another in 1960 and endured a difficult time growing up. At the time of their birth, their mother Ethel had been in the process of divorcing their abusive father Clyde. The pregnancy had influenced Ethel's decision to stay with her husband but within three years Clyde Seabolt was dead, beaten to a pulp during a bar fight of his own making. By then Ethel was fighting her own demons, staring too deeply into the bottle and becoming increasingly erratic and forgetful in her behavior. That meant that she could no longer look after her children and the twins were duly sent to live with an aunt while their three brothers were packed off to their grandparents.

It was hardly the ideal situation but there was one upside to the difficult circumstances that the girls found themselves in. It deepened their bond, drawing them even closer together. By now their respective roles in the sibling relationship were firmly established. Teresa was the sensible one, the one who did well at school and always completed her homework on time; Lisa was the tomboy, always getting up to mischief and relying on her sister to cover for her.

And those roles would be maintained as the girls reached high school. Teresa would excel at her studies and captain the school debating team while Lisa barely maintained a C average. She was more interested in partying, drinking and smoking pot and saying yes to boys when most well brought up girls were saying no. In 1975, at age 15 she decided that she wanted to go back to live with her mother in Bakersfield. Teresa, desperate not to be separated from her sister agreed to go too, but the anticipated family reunion proved to be a pipe dream. Years of alcohol and drug abuse had taken its toll on Ethel and she was in poor health. Two months after the girls moved in she died of a heart attack. Lisa, distraught at the death of the mother she'd never known then tried to kill herself with an overdose of pills.

After the girls graduated high school, Teresa continued to fret over her sister. Lisa seemed to be going down the same path as both their parents, drinking and drugging herself into oblivion and hanging out with a bad crowd. But in 1987, Teresa at last saw a chink of hope in her sister's troubled life. Lisa, now 27, had fallen in love with a young man named Bryce Thomas, two years her junior.

Thomas was not one of the usual cast of deadbeats and addicts that populated Lisa Seabolt's life. He was a solid citizen, an engineer with a good career on the Kern County oil fields. More importantly, he was a good influence on Lisa. She stopped drinking and stopped taking drugs. In October 1987, she gave birth to a daughter named Charlotte and a year later the couple was married. Their second daughter Breana was born in 1992.

But while Lisa Thomas appeared to be living the American dream on the outside, it was an entirely different story behind the walls of the family's Bakersfield home. Lisa had married a man who was the re-embodiment of her father. Bryce Thomas was a bully and a sadist who physically and psychologically abused his wife and was not above battering his little girls. Little by little, he ground Lisa down until she eventually returned to the meth pipe for solace. She stopped eating and began losing weight. Then she began a relationship with a fellow meth-addict and in mid-1996, she walked out on her marriage.

On August 11, 1996, Lisa phoned Teresa and asked if she would look after her girls for a few days while she moved into a new apartment. Teresa of course agreed. She was fond of her nieces and happy that Lisa was removing herself from her toxic marriage. The twins even agreed that they'd take their kids to the beach the following week to celebrate better times ahead. But that date would never happen. When Lisa failed to collect her kids as arranged, Teresa started calling her, becoming more and more concerned with each unanswered call. For all of Lisa's problems, even when she was at the depths of her addiction, Teresa had never known her to be wanting when it came to caring for her daughters.

Eventually, unable to raise Lisa on the phone Teresa called Bryce Thomas. He seemed unsurprised by the turn of events, suggesting that Lisa had probably run away with her drug addict boyfriend. Then he started pouring his heart out, saying how much he missed Lisa and how he wished that they could patch things up. But if this sudden show of sentiment was intended to demonstrate his devotion to his estranged wife, it had the opposite effect on Teresa Seabolt. And that feeling of unease only increased when Thomas showed up to collect his daughters at Teresa's house. His hang-dog expression seemed overblown, somehow put on. Teresa started

wondering if he knew more than he was telling about her sister's
sudden disappearance.

In order to test that theory Teresa decided to do some sleuthing of
her own. She started making some calls, eventually tracking her
sister's boyfriend to the county lockup where he'd been cooling his
heels for several days. "That's when I knew that my sister was
dead," she later recalled. Eight days after Lisa went missing, Teresa
filed a missing persons' report.

But if Theresa Seabolt was counting on the Kern County Sheriff's
Department throwing its weight behind the search for her sister,
she was to be sorely disappointed. Lisa Seabolt was a grown
woman with a history of substance abuse, the police reckoned.
Chances were that she was passed out in some meth house and
would return once her money and drugs ran out. No amount of
asserting that such behavior was out of character could get the
police to take the case seriously.

Frustrated, Teresa decided to take matters into her own hands.
She resolved to confront Thomas directly and demand to know
what had happened to Lisa. When she arrived at his home though,
she found the place empty. That was when she made the decision
to sneak through a window and do a bit of evidence gathering of
her own. She wasn't quite sure what she hoped to find, only that if
something had happened to Lisa in this house there must be clues.
She was unprepared however for what she uncovered. Sliding her
hand between the mattress and box spring in the master bedroom,
she felt her fingers touch something sticky. When she withdrew
the hand she saw that it was covered in blood.

The gruesome discovery spooked Teresa and she decided to leave
immediately. Back at her own house, she dialed 911 and reported
what she'd found. That at least seemed to spark the police into life.
Thomas was brought in for interrogation that same day and

Teresa was sure that he'd be arrested. He wasn't. After asking him to answer some cursory questions, the police let him go. And although they took the bloodstained mattress into evidence, it would be a year before they got around to performing forensic tests on it.

Teresa of course was furious at this outcome. But when she took it up with the Sherriff's department, they told her that they could not initiate a murder inquiry without a body. As for conducting a search for said body, they had no idea where to start and in any case, they weren't even sure that a murder had been committed.

Such official stonewalling might have put off a less determined woman. But not Teresa Seabolt. She'd soon hired a couple of trackers with trained bloodhounds to carry out a sweep, starting at her brother-in-law's house. Then she convinced a local scuba club to carry out searches of local lakes and rivers. When these measures failed to produce a result, she began pestering the lead investigator Sergeant Rosemary Wahl, calling her several times a day. When even that came up empty she went undercover, dressing up in her sister's old miniskirts and halter tops and hanging out with her druggie friends. Someone, somewhere, must know something and if they did, Teresa was determined to find it out.

Her main investigative effort however remained focused on Bryce Thomas. Teresa was certain that there must be something to link him to Lisa's disappearance. One day, while passing by Thomas' house, she spotted his truck in the drive and decided on a whim to check it out. It was a risky proposition. Thomas was a powerfully built man who'd had no qualms in the past about beating up women. Still, there was no stopping Teresa when her mind was made up. And this time her sleuthing efforts paid dividends. Inside the glove compartment, Teresa found a $200 check made out to Lisa. She knew its origin well. She'd given it to Lisa to help her pay her rent. The date was September 11, 1996. The last day that Lisa Thomas was seen alive.

What the check proved was that Bryce Thomas had seen his wife on the day she went missing, something he'd always denied. And with the blood on the mattress (now tested and proven to be Lisa's) and microscopic blood spatters on a wall and drapes in Lisa's bedroom, there was finally enough to charge Thomas with murder. District Attorney Lisa Green did however warn Teresa not to get her hopes up. No one had ever been convicted in Kern county without a body. There was every chance that Thomas would walk free.

Bryce Thomas went on trial for murder on Tuesday, March 3, 1998, with the State's star witness Teresa Seabolt spending over ten hours on the stand, spread over three days. Her testimony would prove crucial in securing the history-making guilty verdict and the sentence of life in prison that accompanied it. There was justice for Teresa's twin at last.

Thomas of course launched an appeal and there were those who felt that he should never have been convicted in the first place, that the State had failed to prove its case beyond a reasonable doubt. Fortunately, Bryce Thomas was about to clear up any misgiving that those skeptics might have been harboring.

While incarcerated at the Lerdo Detention Facility, he began plotting to have Teresa killed, recruiting a fellow inmate to find a hitman for him. To this man he confided details of his gruesome crime. He said that he'd bludgeoned Lisa to death, then driven her body out to the oilfields where he'd placed her in a 55-gallon drum, doused her with gasoline and then kept the fire going until there was "nothing left of her."

Unfortunately for Thomas, he'd failed to heed the old axiom about honor among thieves. The man passed the information on to the police and when Thomas repeated his story to the "hitman" his cellmate had recruited (actually an undercover policeman), the entire conversation was recorded on tape.

Bryce Thomas had an extra twelve years added to his sentence for plotting to murder Teresa. His appeal was also denied. The woman who had brought him to justice meanwhile was named Witness of the Year by the California District Attorneys Association. More importantly, she was awarded permanent custody of Lisa's daughters Charlotte and Breana.

Death of a Fat Man

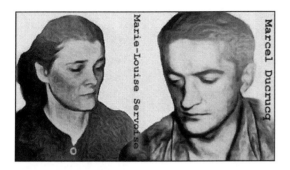

The Hotel Nouvel stood on the Rue de Crimee in the meat-packing district of Paris. The name means "New Hotel" but the Nouvel was neither new nor anything approaching a conventional hotel. It was a ramshackle three-story with a bar on the ground floor and twenty-five pokey residential units above. Its tenants were all long-term residents who earned their coin in the nearby slaughterhouses by day and spent it in the local taverns at night. As a result the Nouvel was a rowdy place, fights were common and screams could be heard at all hours of the day and night. The housekeeper of the establishment, a rotund woman named Yvette Leduc, had long since learned to ignore them.

That is not to say that Madame Leduc was oblivious to the goings-on around her. She was by nature a nosy woman and she kept a beady eye on the Nouvel's denizens. And so when one of them suddenly dropped out of sight in February 1950, she thought it was her duty to inform the local gendarme Jean Labis.

Labis was an interesting character, a hard as nails beat cop who nonetheless seldom had to use his truncheon and fancied himself a bit of a philosopher. He was known for his ability to talk the most violent drunk out of doing something stupid and for dispensing words of wisdom to the troubled. It was known also that he'd sometimes slip a few Francs to the most needy on his regular route. Above all, Labis had a cop's instinct for trouble and when Madame Leduc told him about her missing tenant, he immediately paid attention.

The missing man was Leon Priuer, a truck driver who worked at a local paper disposal plant. Labis knew Priuer well and had occasionally had to throw him in the cooler for drunken behavior or for fighting with his live-in lover Marie-Louise Servoise. He also knew that Priuer was a creature of habit and that his sudden disappearance was out of character. "How long has he been missing?" he asked Madame Leduc.

"I last saw him at around 7:30 on Saturday," the housekeeper replied. "That would be February 11. He was drunk," she added. That meant that Leon Priuer had been missing for four days.

Labis' next move was to trudge up the stairs to the apartment that Priuer shared with Marie-Louise Servoise. Marie-Louise was home but she was in no mood to discuss the whereabouts of her missing lover. "I don't care" she said, blue eyes flashing. "I'm through with him." She then went on to explain that she and Priuer were in the process of ending their relationship and that he would be moving out as soon as another room became available. As for where he might be, Marie-Louise told the officer that he had gone to the country to take care of family business. "At least that is what he told me," she added, drawing her shawl more closely around her. Looking past her into the apartment, Labis noticed that despite the coldness of the day, Marie-Louise had the windows thrown wide open.

Labis had no reason to doubt Marie-Louise's version of events. In fact, it all made perfect sense and would undoubtedly be resolved when the errant Priuer returned from his familial obligations. But something still bothered him and so he decided that he'd go door to door and see if any of the other residents had seen or heard anything. Nobody had but he did get a more complete picture of the missing man. Just about everyone disliked him and more than one person described him as a "drunken bully." The sole exception was a man named Gaston Duplessis who appeared to be Priuer's only friend in the world. "Leon would not have left Paris without letting me know," he said. "If he's missing then something bad has happened to him."

That incidentally, was what Labis was also starting to believe. Troubled by the case, he decided to seek the advice of his station commander, Commissary Louis Covignou. He in turn called in his chief of detectives Chief Inspector Rene Godeau.

Godeau was a large lumbering man whose speed of thought and movement belied his girth. He was known to be a meticulous detective with a near photographic memory. "Priuer?" he said after listening to the story. "Now where have I heard that name?" Then he remembered he'd seen it in the patrol log for February 11. An officer had spotted Priuer, somewhat the worse for drink, standing on a footbridge that crossed the Villette Canal. When approached, Priuer had said that he intended killing himself because "the whole world was against him." The officer had then spent the next fifteen minutes talking him down and eventually Priuer had staggered off. So was it possible that he'd looped around and jumped into the canal after all? Possible, but not likely. Drunks threaten suicide all the time but few of them actually do it. Besides, if Priuer had drowned himself, his body would have turned up by now. Inspector Godeau though that this might be something worth looking into.

Godeau's first step was to question the housekeeper Madame Leduc, and then Priuer's lover Marie-Louise Servoise. From them he got much the same information that Labis had been able to glean. And it was the same when he got around to questioning the other residents. They told him that Priuer was a fat, balding, untidy man with a bad temper, especially when he'd been drinking. They had no idea what Marie-Louise saw in him.

Frustrated, Godeau turned next to Priuer's employer Andre Bloch. "Leon doesn't work here anymore," Bloch informed him. "He resigned."

"Resigned?" Godeau said.

"A good thing too," Bloch continued. "I was about to fire his ass. I'd had just about enough of him turning up to work reeking of booze."

Godeau ignored this outburst. "When you say resigned," he said. "He did this in person?"

"Telephoned," Bloch said. "He spoke to my head bookkeeper."

The bookkeeper Paul Roux remembered the call well. "It was on Monday, February 13 at around 8 a.m.," he said. "He told me he was quitting and that he would send someone to pick up his outstanding pay."

"Why didn't he pick it up himself?" the inspector asked.

"He said that he had a train to catch, family business to attend to."

"And did someone arrive to collect the money?"

Roux said that a man had come in at around ten that same morning. As Priuer had authorized the collection, he handed the money over without question. Godeau then asked Roux to describe the man but the bookkeeper's recollection was extremely vague. "Medium height, medium build, brownish hair, about 25 to 40 I'd say." He did however recall that the man had been wearing blue overalls stained with some brown substance and he'd given off a peculiar, sweetish smell.

"One last thing," Godeau said. "How sure are you that the man who phoned you was Leon Priuer?"

Roux gave a chuckle. "Oh, it was definitely him. We had this thing, you see. Always on payday he'd refer to me as Monsieur Le Banker."

The interview had yielded some interesting information, some of which might have inclined a less tenacious detective to conclude that Priuer had indeed slipped off to the country. But Godeau was not yet satisfied that that was the case. First he wanted to track down the man who'd collected Priuer's pay and he thought he knew exactly where to find him. Roux's description had mentioned a "sweet" odor. Well beside the ubiquitous slaughterhouses in the area, there were also a number of confectioners and chocolatiers. Godeau began checking on those, asking to interview any male employee who was absent from work between 8 a.m. and 11 a.m. on Monday, February 13. His attention quickly fell on a man named Armand Buffet who hadn't shown up at all that day.

Buffet however, had an alibi. He said he'd been hunting near Versailles and was able to provide two witnesses to verify it. But the interview was not entirely wasted. Buffet said that he knew Priuer as they often drank in the same taverns. He also reported that he'd seen Priuer at around 1 a.m. on Sunday morning, standing in the street outside the Nouvel. "He was falling down drunk," Buffet said "staring up at the light from the apartment where he lived and babbling about the love of his life who had waited up for him."

Godeau took his time processing this piece of information. Buffet's account had the ring of truth about it since Priuer had been spotted on the footbridge just an hour earlier by the police officer. And if Priuer was standing outside his apartment at that hour cooing on about his ladylove, then surely he must have gone upstairs.

That theory however was swiftly shot down by Madame Leduc. "The doors get locked at ten," she said. "After that, no one gets in unless I buzz them in and I definitely did not buzz in Monsieur Priuer."

"Could he have got in some other way?" the inspector wanted to know. "Might someone have come in earlier and left the door accidentally unlatched."

"If they did they'd have me to deal with," Madame Leduc said. She did however concede that it was possible.

The investigation had now come full circle. If the theory fermenting in Godeau's brain was right, then Marie-Louise Servoise was lying when she'd told him that Priuer had left never to return. If he was right, then Priuer had entered his apartment drunk in the early morning hours and had been attacked and killed there. But who had killed him? Priuer was a powerfully built man who was known to be violent when he'd been drinking. The petite Marie-Louise would have been no match for him. She must have had help. And who else but the man who had appeared at Priuer's place of work the next day to collect his outstanding wages.

It was a good theory but it still needed to be proved. On a hunch Godeau decided to question Marie-Louise's neighbor, to see if Marie-Louise had received any visitors that night while Priuer was out boozing.

As it turned out, Suzanne Donet had a wealth of information to share. There was no love lost between her and Marie-Louise she admitted, because Marie-Louise had stolen several lovers from her, including Leon Priuer. But Marie-Louise had had a visitor that night. Suzanne hadn't seen the man but she said that she had heard them "going at it" through the walls.

So Marie-Louise had had another lover besides Priuer and Godeau was certain that this man had been her accomplice in murder. He already knew that the man worked in the confectionary industry but what of Marie-Louise, where did she work? A few cursory inquiries revealed that she worked for a confectioner too. Was that where she'd met her lover? There was one way to find out. Godeau called on the plant manager and asked him whether any of his male employees had turned up for work on Monday morning sporting unusual cuts and scratches.

"As a matter of fact, yes," the manager said. "Marcel Ducrucq. I had to pull him off the line and send him to a doctor. I can't have someone working around food with open wounds like that."

"And at what time did he leave to attend the doctor?" Godeau asked.

"About 8:30," the manager said after a moment's thought. "I remember scolding him for taking so long. He was away a good two hours."

Two hours. That would have given him ample time to drop by Priuer's place of work and collect his pay packet. "I need to see this Ducrucq, immediately," Godeau said.

The minute that Ducrucq walked into the office, Godeau instinctively knew that this was his man. He decided to get straight to the point. "I'm from the police," he said. "What did you do with the body?"

"I... I..." Ducrucq stammered, the color blanching from his face.

"It will go harder for you if you hold back information," Godeau snapped.

"I have nothing to say," Ducrucq said, regaining his composure.

"Very well," Godeau said, nodding to the burly sergeant who had accompanied him. "Take him away."

Ducrucq was transported to the police station where he was joined shortly after by Marie-Louise Servoise. Usually male and female prisoners are held separately, but Godeau deliberately shoved them into a cell together and his plan worked. The minute Marie-Louise saw Ducrucq, she blurted out "Leave Marcel alone. He's done nothing. It was me, I killed Priuer."

Over the hours that followed Marie-Louise made a full confession. She said that she had met Marcel Ducrucq two weeks earlier and had fallen in love with him. She was planning on leaving Priuer. On the night of the murder, Priuer had gone out drinking as usual and she and Ducrucq had spent the evening together. She hadn't expected Priuer to return but he had, in the early hours of the morning. He'd become enraged when he'd found her with Ducrucq and had tried to attack her. Ducrucq had then interceded and held him back. While Priuer was thus restrained, she'd picked up a crowbar and struck him on the head. Then after he fell to the ground, she took a scarf and strangled him.

"And what of Priuer's outstanding pay?" Godeau wanted to know. "Who made the call to his employer?"

"That was Marcel," Marie-Louise said. "But I told him to do it. I even told him about Priuer's stupid nickname for the bookkeeper. He owed me that money anyway."

It was a compelling story but not one that convinced Godeau entirely. Why, he wondered, had Marie-Louise had a crowbar at hand? The answer to that question would have to wait. There were more pressing matters at hand.

"You still haven't told me what you did with the body," he said.

"It's probably better that I show you," Marie-Louise replied.

Marie-Louise Servoise was transported back to the Hotel Nouvel in a police van. There she led Inspector Godeau and a contingent of police officers up to her apartment. The window still stood open, allowing in a blast of frigid air but it could not entirely mask the smell of decomposition. In a closet the police made a horrific discovery, a torso wrapped in a bloody blanket. The legs and arms were found in a cupboard under the kitchen sink, while the head was sitting on a closet shelf in the second bedroom, glazed eyes looking down like those of a squat toad.

Marie-Louise Servoise and Marcel Ducrucq went on trial for murder on November 27, 1951. By then, Inspector Godeau's meticulous detection methods had blown Marie-Louise's story out of the water. This was no crime passionnel. This was bloody premeditated murder. The crowbar that Marie-Louise had used to club Priuer and the hacksaw that had been used to cut up his body had been purchased two days before Priuer was killed.

According to Godeau's theory, Marie-Louise had deliberately lured Priuer up to the apartment by leaving the light on, as she always did when she was awaiting his return. Once there she and Ducrucq had overpowered him, beaten him unconscious with the crowbar and then finished the job by strangling him to death. It did not matter who had done the actual killing, both were equally guilty which meant that they'd likely end up on the guillotine.

That terrifying prospect had instantly eroded the "undying bond" Marie-Louise claimed to have with Ducrucq. At trial the lovers quickly turned on each other, attempting to shift the blame. It did them no good. Both were found guilty, although the jury did make a recommendation of mercy.

Marie-Louise Servoise and Marcel Ducrucq were each sentenced to life in prison. Given the prevailing conditions in French penitentiaries during that era, death might have been a better outcome for them.

Taken in the Night

Polly Klaas was a popular girl at Petaluma Junior High in Petaluma, California. The fun-loving 12-year-old was a renowned prankster, always playing some or other hilarious joke on her classmates. She also had a talent for doing imitations. Her rendition of Elvis doing 'Hunka Hunka Burning Love' was legendary while her hilarious imitation of a Chihuahua, complete with protruding tongue and rolling eyes never failed to crack up her friends. And so when Polly invited two of those friends for a sleepover on Friday, October 1, 1993, they jumped at the opportunity. An evening spent in Polly's company was bound to be a blast.

This evening though, was going to be remembered for an entirely different reason. At around 10:45, Polly and her friends were playing a board game in the lounge while her mother and six-year-old sister slept in a back bedroom. That was when a man entered the room, a bearded man with thick wavy hair that fell down to his shoulders. He was holding a knife, so when he told the terrified girls not to make a sound and to do exactly as he said, they obeyed. He then proceeded to tie up Polly's two friends and to pull pillowcases over their heads. Finally, he told them to count to a thousand before making any attempt to free themselves.

The girls however were not about to obey that instruction. The minute they heard the man's footsteps receding and heard the front door latch, they began struggling against their bonds. The knots had been hastily tied and it wasn't long before they were free. That was when the girls removed the pillowcases and saw that Polly was gone. They ran immediately to wake Mrs. Klaas.

Petaluma police officers were soon on the scene and listened intently as the girls told them what had happened and provided a description of the kidnapper. A hunt was immediately launched for Polly and her abductor and was expanded the following day to include hundreds of police officers and civilian volunteers. Meanwhile Petaluma Police Chief Dennis De Witt had assigned twelve detectives to work the case full time, while a hotline was also established to field calls from the public. That was soon inundated with tips and suggestions. None of these got the police any closer to finding Polly or the man who had taken her.

Neither did a substantial reward of $200,000, offered by Hollywood actress Winona Ryder. Ryder had grown up in Petaluma and had taken her first acting classes there. On October 9, she made a public appeal entreating anyone who might know anything to come forward. And plenty of people did respond to the plea, although the fresh deluge of calls all led nowhere.

Then, on October 10, there was hope at last for Polly's distraught parents. A male caller to the hotline said that he had the girl and that she was unharmed. $10,000 in small denomination bills would secure her release. The caller however had been careless, staying on the line long enough for police to run a trace. He was arrested later that day but unfortunately the call had been a hoax. The man had nothing to do with Polly's abduction. He'd been trying to cash in on the situation. That intervention now cost him an arrest for extortion.

The hunt for Polly Klaas meanwhile, was grinding inexorably to a frustrating halt. At its height, 50 police officers and FBI agents had been involved but by October 20, almost all of the Federal agents had been reassigned and the Petaluma task force was down to just eight officers. There were simply no leads to follow. On October 25, a number of Hollywood celebrities raised $30,000 and paid a renowned private investigator to take up the case. His efforts were no more successful than those of the police.

Then on November 28, a most unlikely sleuth provided the break that the police had been waiting for. Laurie Berk, a 40-year-old Santa Rosa resident was walking on her ranch when she found some items discarded in high grass. These included a dark adult-sized sweatshirt, a few strips of cloth and what appeared to be a used condom. Laurie thought she knew who'd put the items there.

A couple of months earlier on the evening of October 1, she'd taken a late night stroll and had encountered a stranger in the exact spot where these items now lay. The man had pointed to his car standing a few feet away and had said that he'd accidentally spun off the road. Something about the man had spooked Laurie and so she hadn't pressed the issue. Instead, she'd hurried back to her house and called the police to report a trespasser on her property. She was uncertain whether a unit had been dispatched to attend to her complaint. Now however, she wondered if the strange encounter might have had something to do with the Polly Klaas disappearance, which had happened that same night. She thought that it might be worth a call to the police.

Sergeant Mike McManus was initially skeptical when he fielded the call from Laurie Berk. But he decided to check it out anyway. It wasn't as though the police were exactly inundated with clues. After photographing and bagging the evidence, he returned to the station and began going through police logs for that night, looking for the trespassing complaint.

As it turned out Sonoma County deputies had responded to the call and had found a man standing at the side of the road at 12:08. They had stopped to question him and he'd immediately aroused suspicion by telling the officers that he had been out sightseeing and that his vehicle had spun out of control and left the road. "Sightseeing?" one of the deputies wanted to know, "At midnight?"

"I have trouble sleeping," the man had explained.

The explanation sounded dubious but with no real reason to detain the man, the officers had let him go. They had however logged his name – Richard Allen Davis. Now, as McManus began looking into Davis' background he realized that Davis had an extensive police record, including arrests for just about every major crime on the statute books. He'd done time for assault, sexual assault, burglary and armed robbery, he'd been a murder suspect in the death of his girlfriend and he'd been convicted of kidnapping. And that was only scratching the surface of a record that included dozens of arrests and several periods of incarceration. But it was the kidnapping conviction that held McManus' attention. Davis had done this before.

McManus' next step was to contact the Petaluma police. They in turn passed on the new evidence to the FBI for analysis. A couple of days later the results were in. The strips of cloth that Laurie Berk had found were a match to the strips used to tie up Polly's friends.

On November 30, two months after Polly Klaas was abducted, a joint force of police and FBI agents raided a house on the Coyote Valley Reservation near Modesto, and took Richard Allen Davis into custody. Davis, who believed that he was being arrested for a parole violation offered no resistance. And he was incredulous when detectives began questioning him about the disappearance of Polly Klaas. He claimed that he did not know what they were talking about and denied even hearing about the kidnapping, this despite the case receiving virtual blanket news coverage in California.

Despite his denials though, the evidence against Davis was stacking up. First Polly's sleepover friends picked him out of a lineup. Then the FBI matched a palm print found at the Klaas residence to Davis. Confronted with this new evidence, Davis eventually cracked. He asked detectives for a pencil and a sheet of paper and drew a crude map, embellishing it with a large 'X'. "She's here," he said.

Later that day, Davis led a convoy of police vehicles to a wooded area some 35 miles north of Petaluma. There under a pile of brush and branches they discovered the mummified remains of Polly Klaas, still dressed in the pajamas she'd been wearing when she was abducted two months earlier. The victim was found. Now came the complex task of bringing her killer to justice.

But Davis was not going to make it easy for them. He'd spent most of his life in the legal system and he knew how to manipulate it. His statements were contradictory and self-serving, seeking to minimize his culpability. He said that he was high on booze and drugs on the night that he took Polly, so high that there were gaps in his memory. He did recall that he had watched Polly and her friends through a window for some time before deciding to abduct one of them. He also remembered that he had Polly hidden in the bushes while he was being questioned by the Sonoma County deputies, although he claimed that she was neither bound nor gagged and could have run away or called out at any time. After the officers left, he took Polly to an abandoned sawmill where he said that he 'must have strangled her,' although his recollection was vague. He gave no reason for the abduction and murder and emphatically denied raping the girl, even though the used condom found at the scene and his record of sexual assault suggested otherwise.

In the end though, Davis' denials did him no good. Brought before a jury in San Jose, where the trial had been moved at the request of the defense, he was found guilty and sentenced to death. Yet even then Davis' reaction sparked outrage. Speaking before sentence was passed he claimed that he had not raped Polly because she had begged him not to 'do me like my Dad does,' the implication being that Polly's father had sexually molested her. It was a hateful thing to say to a family already grieving the loss of a beloved daughter.

Over 1,500 people attended Polly Klaas' funeral, including California governor Pete Wilson and singers Joan Baez and Linda Ronstadt, who performed several of Polly's favorite songs. There was also a message from President Bill Clinton, which was read out at the ceremony.

Polly's tragic death also gave impetus to the 'Three Strikes You're Out' law, which was then before legislators. That law has of course been enacted now and means that any person who is convicted of three felonies is given an automatic life sentence. Had it been in place on October 1, 1993, Richard Allen Davis would not have been free to snatch Polly from her home and snuff out her young life. As it is, he currently sits on death row at San Quentin awaiting his date with the executioner.

Lesbian Vampire Killers

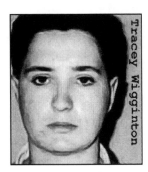

Vampires are real. We've seen them on the screens of our TV's.
And not in some B-rated 70s horror movie or in some tepid
modern incarnation where vampires are good and they sparkle.
We've seen them on the news with blood on their chins – Richard
Trenton Chase of Sacramento, Kuno Hofmann of Nuremberg, Nico
Claux of Paris. And now to this unholy catalog of all too human
monsters can be added another, a six-foot-tall, black-clad Amazon
named Tracey Wigginton who called Brisbane, Australia her
hunting ground.

Tracey Wigginton was born in 1965 and grew up in the northern
Australian coastal city of Rockhampton. Hers was (or at least
should have been) a world of privilege. Her grandfather George
Wigginton was a self-made millionaire and was so admired in
Rockhampton that they named a street after him. When he and his
wife Avril adopted Tracey in 1968 (due to her mother's
shortcomings as a parent), Tracey's future should have been
assured.

But behind closed doors, George and Avril Wigginton were far
from the pillars of the community that they pretended to be.
George was a pedophile, who began sexually assaulting his

granddaughter from the time she reached eleven. Avril meanwhile, was a somewhat neurotic woman who doted on her pet Chihuahuas but hated her husband and frequently took out her frustrations on Tracey, delivering savage beatings with a length of electrical cord. And when Tracey was not herself at the wrong end of a beating, she was forced to watch as Avril delivered a thrashing to Michelle, another girl who the couple had adopted. On other occasions, Michelle was ejected from the house and told to sleep outside with the dogs. She eventually ran away from home at 15, leaving the eight-year-old Tracey to Avril's not so tender mercies.

Given this background of abuse and violence, it is probably no surprise that Tracey acted out at school. By her teens she towered over her classmates and used her size to intimidate them. Already sure by now of her sexuality, she began forcibly molesting other girls, something that saw her expelled from the posh private school she'd been attending. Her grandparents then placed her in a Catholic convent school but she lasted there only a couple of years before being expelled.

Tracey was now 16 years old and living at home with Avril, since George had passed on two years earlier from cancer. And when Avril died in 1981, Tracey's guardianship passed unofficially to a male family friend who was every bit as cruel as Avril had been. Tracey however was not about to stand for any more abuse. She fought back, beating the man so severely that he was hospitalized with head injuries. Thereafter Tracey was on her own. And she continued to make bad decisions.

At sixteen she had an affair with a friend's husband, fell pregnant and had an abortion. At eighteen she received the first installment of her inheritance from her grandparents' estate. The $75,000 windfall was quickly splurged on partying and booze and a motorcycle.

Tracey had by now grown to be an imposing figure, tipping the scales at 210 pounds and standing at just over six feet tall. Not only that but she favored a Goth look of leather jacket, black jeans and dark makeup. After blowing her inheritance she moved to Brisbane, where she worked for a time as a prostitute. But then she found true love in the form of a woman named Sunshine, who she eventually married in a civil ceremony.

In 1986, the 21-year-old Tracey came into the second installment of her inheritance – $80,000 this time. As before the money was spent in record time on trivialities. Two years later Tracey's relationship with Sunshine broke down and the couple separated. A short while later Tracey hooked up with 23-year-old Lisa Ptaschinski and they started hanging out with another lesbian couple, Kim Jervis and Tracey Waugh. The quartet soon discovered that they had a lot in common, specifically an interest in vampires and the occult.

There can be little doubt that Tracey Wigginton was the leader of the group, impressing her gullible cohorts with her shocking claims and outpourings. She professed that she never ate solid food and sustained herself solely on pig and cow blood, which she bought from a local butcher. While this was undoubtedly a gross exaggeration, the naïve Jervis and Waugh were deeply in awe of their de facto leader. Ptaschinski meanwhile was so much in love that she'd do just about anything Tracey asked of her. A chronic self-harmer, she'd been admitted to hospital dozens of times with slashed wrists or to be treated for overdoses. When Wigginton started asking her to cut herself so that she could lick up the blood, Ptaschinski happily obliged.

But Wigginton had darker desires even than that. She often confided in her three proselytes her desire to slash a man's throat and sup on his blood. On the evening of October 20, 1989, as the four sat quaffing champagne at a bar called L'Amour, she was holding court on that familiar theme. Eventually she convinced her friends that tonight was the night that talk became action. At around 11:30, the four of them left the bar and began cruising the streets in Wigginton's green Holden Commodore, looking for a likely victim.

Like Tracey Wigginton and her friends, Edward Baldock had been out for a night on the town. The 47-year-old father of five had been drinking at the Caledonian Club in Kangaroo Point and had left the premises somewhat the worse for drink. He was stumbling along a road in the hope of finding a taxi, when a car pulled up and a young woman leaned out and offered him a ride. She insinuated that there might even be sex involved if he was up to it.

Baldock was obviously happy to accept the ride from the four young women and despite his inebriated state, he gladly agreed to drive with them to Orleigh Park. There, Wigginton invited him to walk with her down to the banks of the Brisbane River, which runs through the park. The other three women initially remained in the car but a short while later, Wigginton returned and asked Ptaschinski to join her, saying she was going to need some help. The two of them then disappeared into the darkness while Jervis and Waugh remained with the vehicle.

Down by the riverbank Baldock was still waiting, swaying unsteadily, when Wigginton and Ptaschinski returned. Wigginton then suggested that he take off his clothes and encouraged him by starting to do the same. Meanwhile Ptaschinski had circled behind Baldock and was approaching on his blindside, holding a knife. On a signal from Wigginton she raised the blade and at that moment, Baldock turned and saw her.

For a moment Ptaschinski just stood there, rooted to the spot. But that moment was all that Tracey Wigginton needed. She drew her own weapon, a wickedly serrated hunting knife and closed in on Baldock. "What are you doing?" Baldock managed to slur before

Wigginton was on him. Ptaschinski meanwhile had dropped her weapon and fled the scene.

The first thrust of the knife caught Edward Baldock in the side of the throat. The second sliced through his fingers, cutting to the bone as he tried to protect himself. Then Wigginton stabbed him again, the knife entering the other side of the neck this time. Blow after blow followed, delivered in a frenzy of steel that severed Baldock's spinal cord and almost decapitated him. By the time the attack was done he had suffered twenty-seven vicious slashes to his face and neck. Wigginton then sat and calmly smoked a cigarette and then walked to the river and washed the blood from her hands, arms and face. She then returned to the car and encouraged her friends to come and view her handiwork. Jervis and Ptaschinski eventually did but Waugh refused and remained in the car. Later as they were driving home, Wigginton confessed to them that as Baldock lay dying, she'd buried her face in his neck and lapped up his blood.

Edward Baldock's body was discovered the following day and it didn't take long for the police to identify a suspect. Inside one of Baldock's shoes, placed under his neatly folded clothes, investigators found a bank card belonging to Tracey Wigginton. No one has ever been able to explain how it got there but it has been speculated that Wigginton dropped it and that when she returned to the car to fetch Ptaschinski, Baldock picked it up and assuming it was his, stuffed it into his shoe for safekeeping.

Either way Edward Baldock had just solved his own murder. Police officers were soon knocking at Tracey Wigginton's door. Questioned about her whereabouts the previous evening, she readily admitted that she'd been down by the river but denied having anything to do with the murder. She suggested that she must have lost the card and Baldock had likely picked it up. And the officers were at first inclined to believe that version of events. None of them had ever seen such a brutal murder and they found it hard to believe that it could have been committed by a woman, even a woman as tall and strongly-built as Wigginton.

However a search of Wigginton's car soon gave them pause for thought. Inside they found a bloodstained towel that Wigginton could not provide an explanation for. In the meantime, the case had taken another dramatic turn as a hysterical Lisa Ptaschinski walked into a police station and confessed all, naming her lover as the killer. Confronted with that confession, Wigginton finally admitted her involvement in the attack, retelling the whole bloody saga with not a hint of remorse.

The police now had forensic evidence, a signed confession and eyewitness testimony. But trying Tracey Wigginton for murder was never going to be the slam dunk that it appeared. That was because a psychiatrist who examined Wigginton was convinced that she was suffering from a severe case of multiple personality disorder and therefore not responsible for her actions.

In the end though Wigginton was declared fit to stand trial and in January 1991, she made it easy for prosecutors by pleading guilty to first-degree murder. After a trial that lasted a mere nine minutes, she was sentenced to life in prison.

Lisa Ptaschinski was also convicted of murder and was sentenced to life imprisonment, while Kim Jervis was found guilty of manslaughter and got eighteen years. Tracey Waugh, who had remained in the car throughout, was acquitted on all charges.

All of the 'vampire killers' have since been released – Jervis in 2003, Ptaschinski in 2008, and finally Tracey Wigginton early in 2012. Upon her release, she expressed remorse for the killing and said that it would forever haunt her.

"I can still smell the river," she said, "the smell of blood, the smell of metal that has been left to rust in the rain. I started to stab him. You think nothing. Nothing goes through your mind. There is no emotion, just blind fury. But once I started I couldn't stop. I couldn't see Mr. Baldock, I kept seeing my grandmother, my grandfather, my mother, my father, and all the people in my life who had hurt me. It was such blind fury I was able to pick a dead man up with two knives. Afterwards, I sat down against the roller door with my arms resting on my knees. I was like a husk, or the shell of a volcano. The public has no idea what my dreams are like at night-time. It's never over. I don't think about it constantly, but whenever I'm alone or having a quiet moment, I think about it and then I cry. Murder is a terrifying experience. It's extremely scary to have that much power. It's playing God with life and death. Nobody should have that sort of power ... but we all do."

Somebody's Mother, Somebody's Wife

Monday, July 29, 1996, was Nathan Streyle's second birthday and his family was planning a special celebration for that evening. Already Nathan's family had given him his birthday present, a blue vinyl teepee which he absolutely loved. Now though Nathan's mom Piper had to get him and his three-year-old sister Shaina off to their babysitter, so that she could head to her job at the Southeastern Children's Center in Sioux Falls, South Dakota. Her husband Vance, 29, had left the family home three hours earlier for his plumbing job.

But today would be no ordinary day in the Streyle household and neither would it culminate in the happy occasion that the family had planned. At around 9:30 a.m., a man entered the family's trailer and overpowered Piper after a brief and violent struggle. Then he dragged the helpless woman to the Ford Bronco truck he had parked outside while her children screamed and begged him to leave their mom alone. Piper Streyle would never be seen again.

The first inkling that something was wrong came around 3 p.m. that afternoon when Patty Sinclair, a colleague of Piper's called to find out if she was okay. Piper of course had failed to show up at work and Patty was worried. Imagine her surprise when Shaina picked up the phone, said that she thought her mom was dead and then promptly hung up. Patty called back immediately and was even more concerned when Shaina said that her mom had left with a man in a black car. Then the little girl started sobbing hysterically, repeating over and over that she did not want her parents to die.

Patty Sinclair was of course an experienced childminder and so she managed to soothe the little girl and keep her on the line while she alerted a co-worker and told her to call the police. Forty-five minutes later, and with Patty still trying to soothe the traumatized little girl, Sheriff Gene Taylor pulled up outside the Streyle's residence. The door stood open and so Taylor entered, noticing immediately that the living area was in a state of disarray. He then walked to the rear of the trailer where he found Shaina with the phone receiver in her hand, crying but unhurt. Two-year-old Nathan was also unharmed but he appeared to be in a dazed state.

By now Vance Streyle had been alerted to his wife's disappearance and was racing home, arriving at around six. In the interim Sheriff Taylor had managed to coax some of the story out of Shaina. She told him that a "mean man" had come into the trailer, argued with her mother and then fired a gun. Her mom had shouted for her and Nathan to run and hide as the man had grabbed her and taken her away in his black car. The little girl also recalled that the man had taken Nathan's birthday present with him.

Shaina had just finished telling her story when Vance arrived home. She immediately threw herself into her father's arms and began sobbing that her mom was going to die. All Vance could do was comfort his children and assure them that the police would do everything they could to bring their mom back safely. Questioned as to who might have wanted to harm Piper, Vance was at a loss. His wife was a kind-hearted, church-going woman. He could not think of a single person who might have borne a grudge against her.

But three days after Piper was taken, Vance did remember something. A few days prior to Piper's abduction, a man had shown up at their trailer to enquire about enrolling his kids in a bible camp that Vance and Piper ran. Piper had explained that the camp was over for the summer but had suggested he sign his kids up for the next year. The man had then left his details which Vance still had. He'd given his name as Robert Anderson.

The police immediately got to work tracking down the man. He was 26-year-old Robert Leroy Anderson and he worked as a maintenance man at the John Morrell meat packing plant. Investigators noted with interest that he owned a dark-colored Ford Bronco; similar to one several eyewitnesses had seen outside the Streyle's trailer on the day of the abduction. It wasn't black though but blue.

On July 30, investigators contacted Anderson and asked him to come down to the police station to be interviewed. Anderson readily agreed and endured eight hours of questioning, during which he stuck unwaveringly to his story. He admitted to visiting the trailer to ask about the bible camp and admitted also that he stopped by on the day that Piper went missing. His purpose was to ask them if he could use the archery range on their property, but after knocking for a while and getting no reply he'd left. He denied knowing anything about Piper's abduction or about her whereabouts.

The police however were never going to take Robert Anderson at his word. They obtained a warrant for his truck and it wasn't long before the evidence started stacking up against him. First they found receipts for duct tape, black water-based paint, paintbrushes and a bucket, all of which had been purchased in the days prior to Piper's disappearance. Investigators immediately suspected that the paint had been used to disguise Anderson's

Bronco and so it proved. Forensics experts found traces of the black paint still clinging to the truck's bodywork. Anderson had obviously tried to wash it off but had made a poor job of doing so.

Also inside the Bronco, investigators found even more incriminating evidence, including a wooden platform with holes drilled into it. This they believed was a restraining device. The holes were perfectly placed so that a length of chain or rope could be looped through to secure a person's wrists and ankles. The proportions of this platform perfectly fit the bed of the truck.

Certain now that Robert Anderson was their man, the investigators expanded their search to the suspect's house. There the forensics kept stacking up – a dirty shovel, furniture moving straps, weeds, a toolbox and dog hairs similar to those of the Streyle's pet would all be used to link Anderson to Piper's abduction. Additionally, there were spots of blood and a semen stain on a pair of jeans. Most telling of all was a blonde hair lifted from the restraint board. It would provide a genetic match to the missing woman.

For now though, that link had not yet been made and with no grounds to hold him, Anderson was released. It would be only a brief respite. After both Vance and Shaina Streyle picked his picture from a photo array, Anderson was rearrested. On August 2, 1996, he was charged with two counts of kidnapping. For now the murder charge would have to wait. The police did not have a body.

But they were determined to rectify that situation. During September 1996, a massive search was launched hoping to find Piper Streyle, or at least evidence that would allow the police to charge Anderson with her murder. That search, employing hundreds of police and civilian volunteers would ultimately prove unsuccessful. Piper Streyle would never be found but that is not to say that the excursion left the police empty handed. In the woods along the Big Sioux River, a searcher found half of a striped shirt similar to the one Piper had been wearing when she was taken. They also found half a roll of duct tape with human hairs attached to it. These would later be matched to samples taken from Piper's hairbrush. Moreover, the duct tape matched the roll recovered from Anderson's truck two months earlier.

There were other finds too, including several lengths of rope and chain, eyebolts, a vibrator and a half burned candle. Tying all of this evidence together, investigators believed that after kidnapping Piper, Anderson had driven her into the woods where he'd taped her mouth and then chained her to his restraint board. He'd then taken his time raping her and torturing her with the vibrator and candle. Then after tiring of his sick game, he'd killed her and then disposed of the body, probably by throwing it in the river.

But that theory, though compelling could not be proven. When Anderson went on trial in May 1997, the charge was kidnapping, not murder. Found guilty, he was sentenced to life imprisonment at the South Dakota State Penitentiary. The possibility of parole was not ruled out and that perhaps, is what motivated investigators to keep delving into Anderson's past, hoping to find the evidence that would keep him behind bars forever. They soon found a lifelong friend of Anderson's, Jamie Hammer, who was prepared to talk.

According to Hammer, Anderson's obsession with torturing and murdering women went as far back as high school. He admitted that he too had been intrigued by the idea and said that he and Anderson had gone as far as planning "the perfect crime." They'd driven out to a desolate stretch of road and scattered "tire poppers" on the blacktop. Then they'd hidden in the woods, waiting for some unsuspecting woman to drive by and suffer a puncture.

Unbeknownst to Hammer, Anderson had a particular victim in
mind, a woman named Amy Anderson (no relation) who he knew
regularly traveled this stretch of road. In November 1994, Amy did
indeed drive over the tire poppers and had to stop with a flat.
Anderson then emerged from the trees and tried to abduct her but
Amy fought him off and managed to escape, after flagging down
another motorist. The case remained unsolved until Anderson
went on trial for Piper Streyle's kidnapping. Then Amy saw his
picture in the paper and contacted the police. She was later able to
pick Anderson out of a lineup.

Anderson's first foray into kidnapping had failed but he remained
as determined as ever to capture a woman on whom he could act
out the sick fantasies whirling around his brain. For his second
attempt he chose a different accomplice, a co-worker at the
Morrell meat packing plant named Glen Marcus Walker. The victim
that they picked was another of their colleagues, a 29-year-old
Ukrainian immigrant named Larisa Dumansky.

Larisa had moved to the United States with her husband Bill in
1991. Initially the couple had both worked at John Morrell but Bill
had found work elsewhere, while Larisa had stayed on, usually
working the night shift. This was the perfect opportunity for a man
like Robert Leroy Anderson. He'd first befriended the woman, then
begun stalking her, learning her habits. Then he'd employed his
tire popper trick, but that had failed because Larisa was afraid to
stop at night in an isolated area and had continued driving on flats.
Finally Anderson had employed the direct approach.

He and Walker confronted Larisa in the parking lot after she
finished her shift. The terrified woman was forced at knifepoint
into Anderson's vehicle. Then he and Walker drove her to Lake
Vermillion where she was dragged from the vehicle and
repeatedly raped. All of her pleas for mercy fell on deaf ears as

Anderson eventually strangled her and then buried her in a shallow grave. It would later be determined that Larisa Dumansky was six weeks pregnant at the time of her death.

In May 1997, shortly after Anderson was convicted for kidnapping, Walker struck a deal with the authorities and agreed to lead them to Larisa's unmarked grave at Lake Vermillion. In the meanwhile investigators had received corroborating evidence from another source, Anderson's cellmate Jeremy Brunner.

According to Brunner, Anderson constantly and in great detail boasted about raping and killing Piper and Larisa. These were not empty boasts either. The detail he provided could only have been known to the killer. For example, he told Brunner that after strangling Piper he'd wrapped her body in "the brat's blue tent" and threw it in the river. He also told Brunner that he'd kept souvenirs from his victims and stashed them in his grandmother's basement. The police would later search this location and recover a ring belonging to Piper and a necklace that had belonged to Larisa.

Robert Anderson was charged with the murders of Larisa Dumansky and Piper Streyle on September 4, 1997, and appeared before the Minnehaha County Circuit Court in March 1999. On April 6th, a jury of eight men and eight women found him guilty on charges of kidnapping, rape and murder. Three days later, the same jury recommended that he be put to death by lethal injection.

Anderson however would never keep his date with the executioner. On March 30, 2003, he was found hanging by a sheet tied to the bars of his cell. The heartless killer had become increasingly despondent after the death of his father, also by suicide three months earlier.

Web of Lies

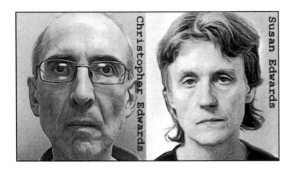

It started as so many family feuds do, with a dispute over money. Susan Edwards had been left a small bequest by her step-grandmother, a sum of £5,000. That money had never reached Susan. Her parents had used it, along with the rest of the estate's proceeds to invest in a London property. Susan however was unconcerned. She didn't particularly need the cash and property values were on the rise. At the time it seemed like a good investment, especially as her parents promised to pay back the £5,000, plus any capital appreciation when they sold the house.

That sale occurred when Susan's father William Wycherley retired and he and his wife Patricia decided to move to the small town of Mansfield in Nottinghamshire. By then relations between Susan and her parents had soured somewhat, particularly over their objections to Susan's choice of husband. The Wycherleys just did not think that Christopher Edwards was good enough for their daughter.

But the real bone of contention was the profit realized on the London property. This was substantial. Even after William and Patricia invested some of their profit in a new house in Mansfield, there remained a sum of over £200,000. Susan quite naturally wanted her share but her father turned out to be a tardy payer. He fobbed her off, saying that he and his wife needed the money for their retirement and that he'd pay Susan when he was able. Eventually after a few heated arguments, Susan stopped asking.

She hadn't entirely given up on her money though. She continued to complain bitterly to her husband. He in turn fanned the flames by bemoaning the unfairness of it all. Eventually, after months of egging each other on the couple decided that the situation needed to be brought to a resolution. And since William Wycherley had steadfastly refused to pay his daughter what was rightfully hers, Susan decided that her parents would have to die.

The reasoning that the Edwards followed in planning the murder could hardly be faulted. Susan's parents were an insular couple who had no friends and no close family ties. They were essentially homebound, neither socializing outside their home nor entertaining guests. If they were to suddenly disappear no one would be any the wiser, particularly if the Edwards were diligent in carrying through on their murder scheme. Their plan was to kill the elderly couple and then keep up the pretense that they were alive.

So it was that on the May Day weekend of 1998, Susan Edwards and her husband traveled to the Mansfield home of her parents, ostensibly for a visit. Sometime during the course of that weekend William and Patricia Wycherley were killed, executed by Christopher Edwards with a World War Two .38 revolver that he owned. On May 1 Edwards was seen by a neighbor in the garden of the property, standing waist-deep in a hole that he'd dug. During the early hours of the following morning, he and Susan dragged her parents' bodies outdoors and buried them one atop the other. The following day Susan Edwards withdrew £40,000 from her father's bank account.

Susan had believed that the disappearance of her parents would go unnoticed and she would be proven right in that assumption. Over the years that followed, she and her husband maintained an audacious web of lies to make it appear that the reclusive elderly couple was still among the living. They canceled newspaper and milk deliveries so that those would not stack up on the doorstep. They traveled fortnightly from their home in Dagenham, east London, to cut the lawn and make it appear that the property was being maintained. They checked on mail, canceled hospital appointments and cashed pension checks. They paid telephone and utility bills. At Christmas they sent out cards to relatives, some purportedly penned by the dead couple, others written by Susan on their behalf. On the rare occasions that someone enquired about the Wycherley's whereabouts, Susan said they were traveling around Ireland or in Morecambe or Blackpool.

It was a massive deception to maintain but the Edwards pulled it off easily and were handsomely rewarded for their efforts. Susan's initial gripe had been over a sum of £5,000. The amount that she drew from her parents' savings and from cashing their pension checks would eventually exceed £245,000.

Then in 2005 an event occurred which spooked the couple into making their first mistake. An accident happened outside the Blenheim Close property, during which a driver veered off the road and crashed through the garden fence. The car came to rest just a few feet from the unmarked grave, churning up the turf as it skidded to a grinding halt. Soon there were police officers traipsing through the garden and a call summoned Susan and Christopher to the scene.

The police had no cause to disbelieve Susan's assertion that her parents were traveling in Ireland and could not be reached. But the incident had shaken her up and she decided that it was time to sell the property. She and Christopher were in any case deep in debt, having blown their ill-gotten fortune on trivialities. The

Edwards were obsessed with celebrities and movie stars and had spent all of their spare cash on memorabilia. The jewel in their collection was a typed letter bearing the signature of Hollywood legend Gary Cooper. There were also items signed by Frank Sinatra and Gerard Depardieu.

The upshot of this reckless expenditure was that the Edwards were dead broke. The sale of the Mansfield property, facilitated by forging William Wycherley's signature rectified that situation for a time. The property went to an investment buyer who soon had a tenant installed. The Edwards meanwhile retreated to Dagenham, having diverted the Wycherleys' mail there. It would be seven years before an item that arrived through the post would have Susan and Christopher scrambling again.

The letter arrived in September 2012. It was from the Department of Works and Pensions and it congratulated William Wycherley on the occasion of his upcoming 100th birthday. The memo also requested a face-to-face interview with Mr. Wycherley, to be conducted at his residence if necessary.

One can only imagine the panic that this innocent piece of correspondence must have instilled in Susan and Christopher Edwards. Up to now they'd expertly deflected questions regarding the Wycherleys, cashed their pension checks and even sold their house. But no amount of manipulation was going to get them out of this latest bind. Left with no other option, the couple boarded the Eurostar and fled to France, where they rented an apartment in Lille.

But despite recently selling the property in Mansfield, the Edwards were already in financial trouble. Much of that windfall had gone to service their debts and a sizable chunk had been blown on their obsession with celebrity memorabilia. After just a year of living in exile, they were flat broke and about to be thrown out on the street.

In September 2013, Christopher Edwards' stepmother received a call from him asking for a loan. She immediately asked for his whereabouts and said that the police had been asking about him. Edwards then spun her a story, saying that Susan had killed Patricia Wycherley but insisting that it had been in self-defense. According to Edwards, he and Susan had been visiting when Susan's parents had gotten into an argument. During the course of that altercation, Patricia had shot and killed her husband. Susan had then confronted Patricia and a skirmish had broken out, resulting in Patricia Wycherley being fatally wounded. Fearful of how the double homicide would be interpreted by the police, Christopher and Susan had then decided to bury the bodies in the garden.

It was a fanciful tale and one that Edwards' stepmother was not prepared to believe. Shortly after hanging up the phone she called the police. An evacuation of the garden at the Blenheim Close property would later unearth the bodies of William and Patricia Wycherley, which had lain buried for over fifteen years. The hunt for their killers was now underway. It would be resolved a month later.

Would Christopher and Susan Edwards have surrendered to the police if they'd had the money to stay on the lam? Probably not. But the couple was in a precarious position, one that had already forced them into selling some of their beloved memorabilia (these pieces had sold for only a fraction of what Christopher and Susan believed they were worth).

In October 2013, the Metropolitan Police received a politely worded e-mail from Christopher Edwards, stating his intention to give himself up. "We are going to surrender ourselves to the UK

Border Force authorities at the Eurostar terminal at Lille Europe station," he wrote. "We would prefer to do this since my wife is already sufficiently frightened." And the Edwards were true to their word, handing themselves over to Customs officials as arranged. They were then transported back to London to be questioned and charged.

Once in custody the killers made no attempt to deny their part in the deaths of William and Patricia. But they stuck steadfastly to the story that Edwards had told his mother, that Patricia had killed William and that Susan had then killed Patricia during a scuffle. Susan also offered a catalyst for the fatal confrontation. She said that her father had sexually abused her as a child and that her mother had admitted to her on the night of the murders that she'd known about the abuse all along but had done nothing to stop it.

Christopher and Susan would stick steadfastly to this story throughout hours of interrogation. But it was soon clear to investigators that the accounts had been rehearsed and honed over many months of preparation. They were just too similar, even employing the same words and phrases when describing the events of that dreadful night.

Susan and Christopher Edwards appeared before the Nottingham Crown Court in June 2014. There, they repeated their story using almost the exact wording that they'd employed under interrogation. Unfortunately for them, the jury found their version of events no more compelling than the police had. Found guilty of two counts of murder, they were each sentenced to a minimum of 25 years in prison.

Thirteen Steps

At around noon on December 15, 1927, a well-dressed young man showed up at Mount Vernon Junior High School in Los Angeles. He said that he was an employee at a bank in the city and that he'd come to collect his boss Perry Parker's daughter. Mr. Parker, he said, had been injured in an accident and was asking for the girl. The teacher who he'd approached with this request was somewhat confused. Perry Parker had two daughters at the school, 12-year-old twins Marion and Marjorie. Which one of the two did he want to see? "The younger one," the man said, then realizing his mistake "the smaller one."

This was a strange request and in any case one that the teacher was not prepared to accede to. The school had a strict policy about releasing its students into the custody of strangers. Nonetheless the young man was adamant, he'd been given strict instructions to collect the child. "Call the bank and verify my credentials," he entreated. "My name is Cooper and I work there as a cashier." And with that the teacher was convinced. The young man seemed genuine enough, he was articulate and respectful and looked her in the eye when he spoke. A few minutes later, Marion Parker was accompanying the man down the path to his waiting Ford Roadster.

The teacher of course had been duped. The young man who'd identified himself as "Cooper" was in fact a 19-year-old miscreant named William Edward Hickman. Not all of his story was a lie though. He had indeed worked at the bank where Perry Parker was a manager, but he'd been fired after he'd been caught committing check fraud. Parker had been a key witness at his trial and although he'd beseeched the judge to go easy on the young man, Hickman had spent a year in juvie. He'd been thirsting for revenge ever since and now he had it in the shape of Parker's young daughter. Parker was going to pay for testifying against him. He was going to pay in mental anguish and cold hard cash.

Marion Parker's abduction did not come to light until that evening when her father returned home from work. When he asked his other daughter Marjorie where Marion was, Marjorie said that a man had collected her from school, apparently on his instructions. Perry Parker had just about processed this startling piece of information when a telegram arrived. "Do positively nothing," it said, "until you receive a special delivery letter."

That letter as it turned out was sitting among the day's mail. Eagerly, Parker ripped it open and had his worst fears confirmed. The letter was ominously headed with the word "Death" and informed him that his daughter had been kidnapped and was being held for ransom. It instructed him to secure $1,500 in denominations of $20. He was then to await further directions. Finally, the letter warned him not to go to the police and threatened harm to Marion if he did so. It was signed "Fate."

The kidnapper had warned Perry Parker not to contact the police but he was not about to comply with that instruction. Immediately after reading the letter he called the Wilshire police station and reported that his daughter had been taken. A bulletin was then distributed, advising patrol officers to be on the lookout for a young man driving a Ford Roadster and accompanied by a girl matching Marion's description. In the meantime, the LAPD's Chief of Detectives Herman Cline took personal charge of the investigation. His first stop was at the Mount Vernon School to question the teacher who had so carelessly released Marion into the custody of a stranger. The woman was understandably distraught but she was able to provide a fairly accurate description of the kidnapper. She said that he was about 5-foot-eight with dark brown hair and hazel eyes. She was wrong about his age though. She estimated it at 28 to 30.

The following day, December 16, a second letter arrived at the Parker residence. Like the first it was headed "Death" but in this one, the kidnapper gave himself an identity.

"Fox is my name, very sly you know," it began. "Get this straight. Your daughter's life hangs by a thread and I have a Gillette ready and able to handle the situation." He then told Parker to be ready to deliver the ransom that night. The letter was signed "Fox-Fate" and below that signature was a plaintive note, written in Marion's hand: "Please Daddy, do what this man tells you or he'll kill me. Please Daddy, I want to come home tonight, Your loving daughter, Marion Parker."

The Parker home was by now under constant police surveillance and a trace had also been placed on the phones in anticipation of the kidnapper's call. That call came early on Friday evening. "This is the Fox speaking," the caller said. "Are you ready to talk business?" Parker assured him that he was. The man then told him to have the ransom money ready and to come in his own car, alone and unarmed. He promised to phone later in the evening to provide the location of the handoff.

At around 8 p.m. the phone at the Parker residence jangled into life again. It was the Fox. "Listen carefully. In exactly fifteen minutes you are to leave your house in your own car. Drive north on Wilton to Tenth, turn right to Gramercy, go one-half block and wait my arrival there. Come alone or the girl dies."

Before Parker could respond, the caller hung up. Plans were then rapidly put in place for officers to follow Parker in an unmarked car. When Parker voiced his misgivings, Chief Cline assured him that they'd tail at a distance and would take no action that might endanger Marion. Parker then agreed.

Unfortunately, the LAPD were not the only ones watching the Parker residence that night. A group of press reporters had been tipped off to the unfolding drama and were parked in the shadows down the block. When Parker set off with his police tail in place, the reporters followed in two vehicles. Then they passed the unmarked police car and fell into convoy behind Parker. This undoubtedly caused the Fox to abort the hand-off. Perry Parker waited in vain at the agreed spot for over an hour before giving up.

The following day there was another special delivery letter from the Fox, this one running to four pages. "You gave me your word of honor as a Christian," he wrote. "And then you try to trap me with the police. Today, Saturday, December 17 is your last chance. If you have not heard from me by 8 p.m., start planning your daughter's funeral. If you want aid against me, ask God, not man." The letter concluded with another note in Marion's child-like hand. In it she pleaded with her father to cooperate fully with the kidnapper. "Please come by yourself," she wrote. "Or you won't see me again."

Perry Parker was understandably distressed by the previous night's events and desperate for the safe return of his daughter. For the second arranged hand-off, he absolutely forbade the police from following him and they to their credit acceded to his wishes. Chief Cline also contacted local newspaper editors and threatened them and their reporters with jail time if there was any more interference in police business.

And so the stage was set. At 7:45 that Saturday evening, the Fox called and directed Parker to a location at the corner of Fifth Avenue and South Manhattan Street. Parker drove to that locale without interference from press or police, and was sitting in his car when a black coupe pulled up beside him. The man at the wheel wore a white handkerchief over his mouth and nose. Parker could see his daughter sitting in the passenger seat, a blanket wrapped around her.

The Fox wound down the window and pointed what appeared to be a sawn-off shotgun through the space. "Hand over the money," he said.

"Is that Marion beside you?"

"Yes," the Fox said. "She's sleeping."

Parker wondered at that. How could his daughter be asleep at a time like this? It was more likely that she'd been chloroformed. She certainly hadn't moved. Still, he didn't argue. He hurriedly handed over the pile of bills. He was eager to hold Marion in his arms again, to know that she was safe.

The Fox meanwhile examined his bounty. Apparently satisfied that it was all there, he turned back to Parker. "Do as I say," he commanded. "I am going to drive down the block a little way and then put the girl out. You are to remain here until you see me drive off. Understood?" Parker nodded. He was prepared to do anything to get his little girl back. Now as he sat and watched, the black coupe trundled halfway down the block before its brake lights flared. Then a door flipped open and Parker saw a bundle thrown from the car into the gutter. He immediately stepped on the gas and raced towards it, standing hard on the brake as he approached, throwing open the door and sprinting towards the pitiful bundle on the ground. It was Marion alright, he could see her mop of dark hair protruding from the blanket. Falling to his knees, he scooped her up and clutched her to him. It was then that the blanket fell away and Perry Parker let out an anguished scream.

Marion, his beloved daughter was dead, mutilated in a most horrific way. Both of her legs had been cut off. So too had her arms below the elbow. Her eyes were wide open, the eyelids apparently sewn to the forehead with black thread. An autopsy would later determine that she'd also been eviscerated, the organs removed and the body cavity stuffed with rags.

The kidnapping of Marion Parker had now escalated into one of the most savage murders anyone could remember. In response, the police launched what would become the largest manhunt ever conducted on the West Coast. And that search was given renewed impetus on Sunday, December 18, when a man walking his dog in Elysian Park discovered newspaper-wrapped packages containing Marion's legs and forearms. By evening there was a bounty out on the killer – $50,000 Dead or Alive – and hundreds of police officers, as well as thousands of enraged citizens had joined the hunt. Their quarry was described as a young white male, about 25 years old, 5 feet 8 inches tall and weighing 150 pounds. He was smooth shaven with dark wavy hair and was believed to be driving a black Ford roadster.

The police got a major break in the case when a towel that had been used to wrap Marion's body was found to have a laundry tag attached. That brought officers to a residential hotel in downtown Los Angeles. More than 100 cops were involved in the search. In one room they encountered a young man who was a good fit for the suspect but much younger at 19. He gave his name as Donald Evans and willingly allowed four officers to search his room, even commenting that he "hoped they would catch the fiend." Shortly after the police concluded their search, Donald Evans, a.k.a. William Hickman, a.k.a. The Fox, checked out of the hotel, stole a green Hudson sedan at gunpoint and drove out of Los Angeles, heading north.

Hickman must have thought that he'd given his pursuers the slip but on Monday December 18, the police caught another break when they found the Ford Roadster he'd used in the kidnapping. Hickman had wiped the car down to get rid of fingerprints but he'd been tardy, leaving one clear print on the vehicle's wing-mirror. That at last gave investigators a name to work with. Their kidnapper, their killer, was a petty thief and sometime forger named William Edward Hickman. Before long, Hickman's mugshot was gracing the front page of every newspaper from L.A. to Chicago to New York.

But where was the fugitive? He was in Seattle, Washington, where on December 21, he passed one of the stolen $20 bills. A day later he was in Portland, Oregon, and on December 22 he used another of the $20 bills to buy a movie ticket in nearby Pendleton. That same afternoon his stolen green Hudson was spotted driving east on the Old Oregon Trail. Officers gave chase and Hickman was soon in custody.

Hickman was extradited to California within the next few days. He readily admitted taking Marion but denied killing her, blaming the murder on an accomplice. Unfortunately for Hickman, the man he named had a cast iron alibi. He was serving a prison term at the time of the abduction and murder. Faced with the mounting evidence against him, Hickman finally broke down and confessed.

He said that it had never been his intention to kill Marion but that he'd realized that she could identify him and had thus "reluctantly" decided to commit the murder. He'd strangled her, he said, while she was tied to a chair. He'd then started dissecting the body in the bath tub but soon realized his mistake. Parker was likely to want to see his daughter before handing over the money. It was then that he'd concocted his bizarre scheme to make it appear that Marion was still alive.

William Hickman went on trial in Los Angeles in January 1928. The case against him was a strong one, with forensics, eyewitness testimony and his own confession. But even then it was unclear whether he'd get the punishment that he so obviously deserved. The previous year, the state of California had legislated the plea of "not guilty by reason of insanity" and this was the approach that Hickman's defense decided to take. After all, few could believe that a man in his right mind could have killed and so horribly mutilated an innocent little girl.

Several experts were asked to examine Hickman and their findings fell neatly along party lines. Those for the defense decreed that Hickman was mad as a hatter; the prosecution experts thought that he was sane and lucid and therefore responsible for his actions. It would be Hickman himself who resolved the impasse.

While awaiting trial, Hickman was spotted by a prison guard passing a note to a fellow inmate. The note was confiscated and once the guard read it he immediately called the District Attorney. The content of the note turned out to be gold to the prosecution.

In it Hickman asks his prison buddy for advice on 'acting mad.' "Should I throw a laughing, screaming fit?" he asks. "Or should I pull some crazy trick on D.A. Keyes." He concludes with a P.S. "You know, and I know, that I am not insane."

Once the note was read out in court, Hickman's fate was effectively sealed. It took the jury just 36 minutes to find him guilty of first-degree murder and in that era, the offense carried a mandatory sentence of death by hanging.

William Hickman went to the gallows at San Quentin State Prison on October 19, 1928. In the weeks running up to his execution he'd been in a jovial mood, assuring warders and fellow prisoners that he was not afraid to die. And he kept up that front right until the last moments of his life. Climbing the 13 steps that led up to the scaffold, he collapsed in fear and had to be carried the final few feet by the guards.

Hickman's death was not the quick neck break usually associated with judicial hangings. The drop had been slightly miscalculated and he was throttled to death, taking ten minutes to die. Ironically, this was the same fate he'd inflicted upon his innocent young victim.

For more True Crime books by Robert Keller
please visit:
http://bit.ly/kellerbooks

Made in the USA
Middletown, DE
27 April 2017